GREAT PLANTS
for SMALL GARDENS

GREAT PLANTS *for* SMALL GARDENS

NIGEL COLBORN

conran
OCTOPUS

First published in 1997 by
Conran Octopus Limited
a part of Octopus Publishing Group
2-4 Heron Quays
London E14 4JP
www.conran-octopus.co.uk

Reprinted in 1998, 2001

British Library Cataloguing-in-Publication Data
A catalogue record for this book is available from
the British Library.

ISBN 1 84091 192 1

COMMISSIONING EDITOR: Stuart Cooper
PROJECT EDITOR: Carole McGlynn
EDITORIAL ASSISTANT: Helen Woodhall
ART EDITOR: Prue Bucknall
ILLUSTRATORS: Shirley Felts, Joanna Logan, Lesley Craig
PICTURE RESEARCH: Helen Fickling
PRODUCTION: Mano Mylvaganam
INDEX: Indexing Specialists

Printed in China

CONTENTS

CHOICES AND CHALLENGES

A small garden need never be a limited garden. Like a painter's canvas, the only restrictions are the physical dimensions and, within its allotted space, anything can happen. A tiny 8cm (3in) etching by Rembrandt uses rather less space and material than does his vast 'Nightwatch' project; a simple ink drawing by Vincent van Gogh may not be as detailed a work as his masterpiece 'The Potato Eaters'; but all four pictures carry more than a full complement of artistic integrity. And similar comparisons can be made with that other art form, the garden. The overbearing designs of the seventeenth century, for example, when vast parterres and complicated knot gardens proclaimed the wealth of their owners, are no more splendid, artistically speaking, than some of today's extraordinary designs for tiny, private town gardens.

Small size does not limit but, rather, presents a different range of possibilities, as far as design is concerned. But there is more! In a small plot, the choice and arrangement of plants to create the finished garden is not merely complementary to its design, it is integral – indeed, in a tiny garden, it is possibly even more important than layout and structure. Without artistic planting, design, however inspired, is useless, ugly, an expensive waste of space. But without good garden design, artistic planting can, to a certain extent, salvage something of value from the dross – even if it does no more than improve the view from the living room window.

The number of plants that will fit into a small space is limited. Correct choice of plants is therefore crucial – every one must be carefully considered, every one must earn its keep. And that is the purpose of this book: to provide suggestions for which plants, out of the sixty thousand or so available to gardeners of temperate or cool climates, make the best possible choice, in the most pleasing combinations, for every kind of small garden.

Above: A small, shaded corner is brought to life by associating woodland plants with varied types of foliage. Ferns (Hart's-tongue fern and soft shield fern) are combined with stinking hellebore (*H. foetidus*) against a mossy background.

Opposite: Even in small spaces, grouping together plants with distinctive leaves helps to create different effects. The architectural leaves of *Hosta sieboldiana* and *Rodgersia pinnata*, both bold, both large-scale, here make an interesting contrast in texture. The soft outline of the pink rodgersia blooms adds a further dimension and introduces colour. The small spaces between these plants have been filled with Welsh poppies (*Meconopsis*).

WHAT IS A SMALL GARDEN?

No space is too small to grow plants. Glib as that may sound, for the purposes of this book we can assume that there is virtually no lower limit on garden size. Some of the plants and plant combinations will make excellent container subjects as well as playing a small role in a larger composition. A collection of decorative thymes, for example, will sit as comfortably in a small alpine sink as on a larger terrace where they might run along cracks in the paving and spread over several square metres. In each chapter, we will look at overall planting schemes and ideas but will then focus on specific combinations and recipes within such schemes.

What is meant by 'small' depends on your point of view. With increasing urbanization around the world, the space allotted to individual gardens seems to shrink with every new development. Nowadays, estate agents call anything with more than, say, a tenth of an acre a large garden. For our purposes, however, it might be more helpful not to consider

actual garden size at all, but to think of planting in terms of furnishing small spaces. That way, we open up possibilities rather than restrict. Whatever your garden size may be – from a few square metres (yards) upwards – there are bound to be key areas or small spaces that demand extreme care in planting. The view from an important window; an outdoor seating area; a problematic corner; a strangely shaped plot – all these come within the scope of this book, whose aim is to help you find absolutely the right combination of great plants for small gardens.

WHAT MAKES IT CHALLENGING?

Limited space is obvious, but when there is so much pressure on that space, especially in a family garden, some desired uses might be in conflict. Children need space to play; adults will want an area in which to relax and, perhaps, to entertain friends; keen plant collectors will need to accommodate their favourite species; the kitchen might call for a supply of fresh food and so on. Fitting all these activities into a small space presents a challenge, but careful planting can overcome many of the obstacles. Food, for example, can be produced from an ornamental as well as a utilitarian garden. Children's play zones can be concealed with attractive screens of climbers and, better still, children can be encouraged to respect, love and enjoy their garden, not only as somewhere in which to let off steam but also a place to enjoy nature.

With such pressure on so small a space, it is not difficult to see how important it is to arrange the planting for best effect. Year-round interest has to be one of the chief objectives, but it will be especially important to enhance the summer displays, since that is the time of year when the garden is most used. It is neither possible nor desirable to strive for a constant display of maximum intensity. Just as with music or drama, a garden must have dynamics – periods of build-up leading to climaxes which will be followed by declines and transitions that, in turn, act as

Below: Rich colour for mid-spring offers plenty to follow. As forget-me-nots (*Myosotis*) and columbines (*Aquilegia*) mature, their pink and blue colours give way to clematis and pink campion (*Silene maritima*) which herald summer. In winter, the evergreen, variegated euonymus makes a pleasing outline in the border.

preludes to the following build-up. In summer, the natural progress of the growing season results in a climax around the longest day. Thereafter, things run downhill, but with skilful planting the decline can be made more gradual, without diluting the strength of the main climactic period. And it is possible to create subsidiary bursts of growth and colour, so that a series of displays carries the year through to late autumn.

Try as you might, winter will be less interesting but some interest is essential and this is the season when certain plants will be working harder to earn their keep than at any other time of year. Shapely winter outline is the key to successful planting and design but you need more than a pretty tree or hedge to complete the winter garden. Small surprises are necessary, tiny serendipitous fragments to reward anyone brave enough to don coat and boots and venture into the cold. A single group of early-blooming snowdrops can do the trick, as can a single twig of *Prunus mume* in full flower, or a touch of hoar frost on a blood-red holly berry. These need to keep coming, week after week, making highlights to the general run of the quiet seasons. Then, as the year gathers warmth and growth begins in earnest, each new event needs to pack a stronger dramatic punch.

The onus, in any small garden, is always on the plants. Plants that are merely good are not up to the demands of the small garden. To contribute fully, every plant must exhibit superlative qualities, whether of character, beauty, fragrance or colour. Such qualities can be termed 'greatness' and therefore the classic garden plants which exhibit them can be called 'great'.

Above: High summer brings a climax in growth and in colour. Plants become overgrown and borders are bright with poppies (*Papaver*), pinks (*Dianthus*), mallows (*Lavatera*), lady's mantle (*Alchemilla mollis*) and, of course, roses. But in autumn and winter, when all this exuberant growth dies down, the background shrubs and trees provide a more distinct outline.

Opposite: A great plant really earns its keep! *Cornus controversa* 'Variegata' is a shrub which looks as lovely in winter outline, with its tiered branches, as it does in summer when in full foliage.

Below: Giving brilliant autumn colour, the dramatic foliage of the oak-leaved hydrangea (*H. quercifolius*) is highlighted here against the adult foliage of cream-variegated ivy.

WHAT IS A GREAT PLANT?

What are the special qualities which separate that distinguished cadre of classic plants from the rest? Gardeners the world over have more than sixty thousand species, varieties, seed strains, forms and cultivars from which to choose. From giant forest trees to tiny moss-like saxifrages and from rampant climbers to diminutive succulents, the range of shapes, sizes, habits, colours, fragrances and other characteristics of individual plants is so diverse that when planting your garden – regardless of conditions and despite limited dimensions – you will always be spoilt for choice.

Within that range, however, lies a selection of plants which tower head and shoulders above the rest – not in physical size, but in quality. These are the great plants, the classics whose contribution to the garden is so much better than average. What makes them great? Character, certainly – distinctive foliage, endearing flower shape, curious seed capsules – but there's more to it than that. To be truly great, a plant must exhibit a number of extra-special characteristics. Some of these are obvious; others are less easy to define but are, nonetheless, essential parts of the great plant's make-up. Wherever you live and however small your garden, these are the plants that will always justify the space they occupy by providing you with constant delight.

SEASON OF INTEREST This means much more, of course, than merely flowering period. Some plants are constantly in flower, but offer little to the well-planted garden, others never bloom and yet are a constant joy. Clearly, a rose that blooms from midsummer to late autumn is likely to score over one that blooms for a couple of weeks around the longest day – unless that short-blooming rose also provides a dazzling display of autumn hips and has graceful, ferny foliage which turns golden-yellow before it falls, to leave a bare-branched shrub with pleasing winter outline. Under those circumstances, the latter is a better choice, because of its constant and changing beauty, than the former which, when out of flower – for eight months at a stretch – contributes nothing.

ARCHITECTURAL QUALITY Winter outline, with shrubs and trees, is essential. Conifers and hollies, with their distinctive shapes, are helpful here, but so too are those priceless plants whose branches spread out in graceful tiers. The dogwood (*Cornus controversa*) is thus a great plant, but so too are such short-term summer plants as *Rheum palmatum*, with its dramatic leaves, and the giant thistle (*Onopordum nervosum*).

FLOWER POWER This hippie term of the 1960s was first applied, with perfect appositeness, to plants by the fluent and erudite English gardening writer, Christopher Lloyd. How much flower a plant displays is important, of course, but timing is also critical. Hellebores, whose large, beautiful blooms appear in midwinter, have twice the 'flower power' of, say, petunias or marigolds which come at a time of flower glut. A late-spring-flowering cherry has less impact than one that gives colour in winter. Staying power is important too, making such genera as *Penstemon* truly great, because they produce a near-constant supply of blooms in the growing season.

COLOUR Colour is crucial – not only that of flower colour, but also of foliage, winter stems, berries and fruits, even of dying blooms and leaves. Hues, whether strong or gentle, should be clean and distinctive – true blues, pure pinks, assertive oranges and reds – or subtle and harmonious. Indeterminate, dirty hues and tones are less likely to please and, in a small garden, flowers in these colours take up too much space for their contribution.

FORM AND VARIETY Almost every plant species has a variation in its forms. Good nurserymen make the best selections and clone them for the commercial market. The North American shrub *Garrya elliptica*, for example, is a handsome evergreen with distinctive winter catkins in the male of the species, but the form 'James Roof' produces much longer catkins than average, and more of them. In a small garden, where space is at a premium, such a selection will ensure a better, longer-lasting display.

Trees and shrubs are long-term, but with such quick-growing plants as hardy annuals, you can make your own selections, based on colour, size or habit. Buy a packet of Californian poppy seed in mixed colours and weed out all the shades you dislike but save seed from your favourite hues. Go for vivid sunset shades or for creamy lemon tones, selecting seed from larger flowers or plants with neater habits.

MANAGEABILITY The greatest plants are those that can fend for themselves. Susceptibility to disease, inability to stand without support, invasiveness or the need for fussy cultural practices detract from a plant's qualities. But some species may be so ravishing that they are worth growing even though they are difficult. The Bourbon rose 'Zéphirine Drouhin', for example, is prone to powdery mildew. But its purple-pink blooms are so sumptuously fragrant, produced for so long, and the thornless plant has such excellent vigour that it is worth growing regardless of the disease, which is never fatal and seldom disfiguring.

Below: Great plants should be robust and trouble-free. Among autumn-blooming perennials, many North American prairie species make a great contribution. Coneflowers (*Rudbeckia*) come in clean, bright colours, mostly in the yellow range, with dark, contrasting centres. They are easy to grow and do best in full sunlight on reasonably rich soil.

FIVE OF THE BEST

***Clematis* 'Bill McKenzie'** A vigorous climber, though easily controlled, with a long season of yellow 'orange-peel' blooms followed by a display of silky seedheads.

Galanthus elwesii Early-flowering species of snowdrop with larger blooms than the common species, and larger foliage. Often comes into bloom within a week of the shortest day.

***Ilex aquifolium* 'Madame Briot'** A superb holly with well-formed leaves, each edged with yellow-cream, colouring bronze in hard weather. The female bears a good crop of red berries. A fine, compact habit when grown naturally, but can be clipped into any shape desired.

***Penstemon* 'Evelyn'** Among the hardiest of the genus, with narrow leaves, herbaceous stems and a continuous succession of narrow, tubular pink flowers throughout the growing season.

VIOLA CORNUTA

Viola cornuta A low-growing, perennial species with mid-blue flowers produced almost throughout the year.

selection of plants that will thrive, given the soil, aspect, climate and so on. But the main thrust of any artistic planting scheme is to use the plants as foundation layers with which to create an overall effect, in exactly the same way as an artist composes a picture. Colour, textures and individual forms will play an important role further along the development process but, first and foremost, it is essential to consider shape or outline.

THE OUTLINE

Outline will be your key consideration when beginning your structural planting. This is the backbone, skeleton or profile of the garden, as visible in winter as in midsummer. It is the framework on which the rest of the planting is to hinge and is therefore likely, in a new garden site, to be the first piece of planting you undertake. In an existing garden, there may already be trees or shrubs which you wish to incorporate into your new scheme. You may also want to create an outline with objects other than plants: walls, pergolas, buildings, gateways, arches and other structures all help to give outline. But since this is largely a book about creative planting, we will focus on using plants as outline features.

Outline plants, which are almost always trees and shrubs, must fulfil several roles, especially in small gardens where space is at a premium. They will provide shelter, particularly if sited on boundaries or positioned in the teeth of the prevailing wind, and are often important for privacy as well. They will probably form a neutral backdrop in summer, when other plants are busy, but will tend to become more central in their winter roles, when the colour and interest have diminished elsewhere. A selection of evergreens will therefore be needed, to sustain winter freshness, and to provide extra shelter for delicate plants. Sometimes they will play host to flowering climbers, or they may be disciplined to create formal shapes in a more geometric garden.

Above: Planting design at its best: a shapely variegated holly for year-round outline, plenty of contrasting foliage in the understorey and vivid crocosmia as a highlight.

Opposite: Clipped box and a bay tree create a strong living profile, softened in winter and spring by the golden-green flowers of *Euphorbia characias*.

PLANTING DESIGN IN A SMALL SPACE

Planting design is a matter of composition, rather than simply finding homes for the plants you may have acquired. It is necessary to view the garden, or the section of the garden to be planted, as a whole and to view it in the context of its surroundings. Practical considerations are important, of course, not only from the point of view of scale and size, but also in the

GREAT OUTLINE PLANTS

Outline trees and shrubs come in a variety of shapes, often distinctive, and all of potential value in creative planting schemes. They may be:

Conical as in *Picea* or Christmas trees

Columnar as in *Carpinus betulus* 'Fastigiata' or *Fagus sylvatica* 'Dawyck'

Rounded as in common holly, or varieties of *Ilex altaclerensis*

Tiered as in *Cornus controversa* or *Viburnum mariesii*

Low domed as in dwarf rhododendrons

Suckering or spreading as in *Mahonia pinnata*

Weeping as in *Sophora japonica* 'Pendula'

Once familiar with the various shapes of the outline plants, it should not be difficult to devise an arrangement of different ones, suited to your specific dimensions and to your tastes. If, for example, you planned to create a sheltering belt of outline plants at one end of your garden, you might place a single specimen, or a trio or group, of fastigiate or columnar trees as a centrepiece, then arrange domed, rounded or tiered plants around these in descending levels.

How you compose your outline depends on the effect you want to achieve. In a naturalistic garden, with informal planting, it is never a bad idea to take a lesson or two from nature, and imitate the contours of a piece of natural landscape. Alternatively, you may decide on a more formal outline, with topiary or clipped hedges, possibly incorporating walls or other man-made structures (covered in more detail on page 39).

You may need to tailor your outline planting to conceal an unsightly object or to hide a neighbouring window that compromises your privacy. You may wish to disguise an entrance to another part of the garden, to heighten the pleasure of a stroll by providing a surprise or simply to make a statement with a favourite tree. Whatever the function of the planting, never forget that the species or variety you select must satisfy as many criteria of 'greatness' as possible.

Above: Understorey plantings can portray a range of different effects. Here, the sombre, strap-like foliage of the dark *Ophiopogon planiscapus* 'Nigrescens' makes a striking contrast in texture and colour with the silver-lined, fresh-looking foliage of *Alchemilla conjuncta*.

THE UNDERSTOREY

Once your plans for the outline planting are in place, the remaining task is to fill in the spaces with what, to take a term from natural history, one might call 'the understorey'. These are the plants that clad most of the landscape – the green mantle which furnishes woodland floors, covers roadside verges, grows along the edges of lakes, streams and river banks. Wherever, in nature, there is neither intensive agriculture nor urbanization, plants take over, creating their own special compositions. Woodland flora, for example, might be coloured with drifts of bluebells in spring or with purple willow herb in summer. Farm headlands – those areas between arable crops and the field edge – might be speckled with primroses or coloured scarlet with wild poppies. Some understoreys are extra special: mountain meadows have their short turf studded with millions of such gorgeous alpine flowers as blue gentians, purple cranesbills, columbines and Indian paintbrushes in gorgeous reds and orange. In a garden, the aim with understorey planting is to take the best from nature and imitate it in microcosm.

It is with the understorey – the infill planting – that most of the mood, colour and style of the planting is set. Plants with different foliage textures or special characteristics can be used to create particular

Below: In this light, bright infill planting, the variegated hostas and white forget-me-nots create the background to the cream and white tulips ('Purissima' and 'Spring Green'), which provide flower interest in spring, backed by the fragrant, globe-shaped blooms of *Viburnum carlesii.*

Above: Azaleas (*Rhododendron* species) provide spring glory with their brilliant hues; they will later tone down to become shapely outline shrubs, but for now the red flowers make a glorious contrast with the natural blue of the bluebells.

effects: in shade, for example, such plants as the lady fern (*Athyrium filix-femina*) introduce a soft, feathery quality which can be enhanced with the broader, bolder foliage of hostas, for instance. The effect can be darkened with the bronze leaves of *Heuchera* 'Palace Purple', making a fine setting for, say, blue Himalayan poppies as highlight plants. Thus a small fragment of wholly natural woodland planting has been created, but using exotic plants from all over the world. In a hot, dry position, even in a formal setting, the silvery foliage of *Santolina neapolitana*, of shrubby helichrysums and the filigree texture of *Artemisia* 'Lambrook Silver' can be teamed with lavender and a selection of pinks to capture the feeling of a rocky, summer-roasted Mediterranean hillside.

With the understorey come most of the opportunities to create special colour schemes and to develop team mates, to arrive at classic combinations which really work, to develop runs of colour which remain constant through the seasons, but with the colours provided by different species. Thus, in a predominantly blue scheme, *Omphalodes verna* or *Brunnera macrophylla* might launch the year in late winter before giving way to blue columbines in later spring, perhaps in association with the large-flowered hybrid clematis 'H.F. Young', followed in summer by *Aster amellus*, *Cynoglossum* or blue *Polemonium*, ending, in autumn, with *Gentiana asclepiadea*.

From a practical point of view, the understorey represents the bulk of your planting – ground cover, for example, is almost all understorey – and therefore you are likely to need larger quantities of the same kinds of plants. It is also with the understorey that much of the labour resides. Maintaining borders, for example, is made easier by using dense plantings of weed-suppressing perennials, but if you prefer the greater drama, the brighter colours or the stronger impact of, say, summer bedding, this will create far more work, as well as adding considerably to the cost of planting and maintaining the garden.

CONTROLLING THE SCALE

Scale – so important in any planting scheme – can be adjusted with understorey plantings. In a very small garden it makes sense to populate the area with plenty of small-stature plants. Not only do these take up less space, they also give the impression of a richer planting, with more variety and a wider selection of different textures, colours and characters. Even on a tiny scale, perhaps in a shallow trough, it is possible to develop a varied planting, along the lines of a miniaturized landscape, using cushion saxifrages, *Sedum spathulifolium* and other small stonecrops. Bulbs could make a valuable contribution here, but it is important to remember scale, and to select only the smallest of the crocus species, miniature varieties of narcissus and so on.

Whatever the scale, the understorey planting must link closely with the outline. The objective is to create a whole picture from the integral parts, so that one's eye will, perhaps, light on the brighter, or more conspicuous, parts – but will then move involuntarily over the whole, taking in the differing shapes of the outline, running the gaze upwards to the highest point. If shapes, colours or arrangements conflict, the general effect will be spoilt and the garden will take on a fussy, uncomfortable appearance. Variegated foliage, for example, can be effective if used with care, but if you place, say, an *Aucuba japonica* 'Crotonifolia' directly under a variegated maple, perhaps next to a cream and green holly with a plum-pink rose to grow through it in summer, the splendid and desirable impact of each plant mentioned is wasted. Worse, the overall effect is so unnatural and uncomfortable as to be almost nauseating.

A final point about the understorey is that nothing in a planting plan is cast in tablets of stone! Your garden structure and dimensions may be fairly rigid and your outline planting of trees and major shrubs difficult to move, once established. But the great feature of understorey planting is that it is fluid. You can make what changes you like, almost when you like, from minor adjustments – creating room for new introductions – to a major re-planting operation to transform an area of the garden. Gardens are a dynamic art form: for many gardeners, the greatest pleasure is derived from changing the plants around.

Above: Small-scale plants form important ground cover. The lesser periwinkle (*Vinca minor*) makes a happy contrast with the leathery leaves of *Bergenia cordifolia*, which turn bronze in frost.

HIGHLIGHT PLANTS

When the outline planting is well established, and the understorey is in place, providing pleasure and interest right through the year, and running through changes in mood and style as one wanders through the garden, there is a final aspect of creative planting that is a central part of every well-tempered garden. The whole dynamic structure of a garden, whatever the style or preferences of the gardener, depends upon a small but choice cadre of plants which will be your garden's highlights − your star performers.

Some of your plants will fulfil a dual role, presenting themselves as focal points at certain times, but later slipping back into the chorus line. Flowering trees − cherries, crab apples, camellias and the like − are the centre of attraction in blossom but every one of them, provided you have selected truly 'great' varieties, will continue to make a huge contribution, albeit in a humbler key, for the rest of the year. Others, like tall lilies in summer, paeonies in late spring, winter bulbs or, perhaps, a showy container planted with hot colours for a terrace display, are there specifically for their short-term brilliance. If you can forgive yet another analogy drawn from the arts, think again of an orchestral work, where a movement progresses towards its climax. There may be a bright phrase or two from the brass section, a crash of cymbals or a loud drum roll, all of which highlight and decorate the main themes or changes in theme or, at any rate, important sections in the music. When you listen, this is often the part that makes the hairs at the back of your neck bristle. And that is the desired effect, visually, to try to achieve in the garden.

Highlight plants are effective in a number of different ways. They create a focal point, cementing together an otherwise diffuse planting scheme. Think, for example, of how a predominantly green ground cover in spring, perhaps consisting largely of *Euphorbia robbiae* and other low to mid-height perennials not yet in bloom, can be given more zest if a bold cluster of red tulips, or perhaps a small colony of the scarlet *Anemone fulgens*, have been placed in their midst. Star performers are great for announcing a new season, too. The arrival of the rose season, for instance, is heralded more loudly if the first rose tree to bloom is one of the especially floriferous species, such as 'Marguerite Hilling' or 'Frühlingsgold'.

Highlight plants can also be used to flag entrances to new parts of the garden, or to beckon from a distance. On an arch or a gateway, the more arresting the plants − especially climbers on the structure itself − the more likely a person is to pause, admire, then to move on. A distant splash of colour, especially if it is half-concealed by such natural or artificial barriers as hedges or trelliswork, will tempt one to move to the spot to find out what the plant is.

PRACTICAL CONSIDERATIONS

Professional horticulturists are rather fond of building more mystique into the craft of gardening than really exists. Apart from certain temperamental species, most plants are straightforward in their requirements and need but minimal skill in their culture. Most of the management work you do in your garden is a matter of common sense. Once you understand that soil is a living layer, with a balance of air, water, minerals, rotting organic matter and a myriad micro-organisms, and that, in nature, plants derive minerals and water from the soil but manufacture their bodies − leaves, stem and root − from carbon dioxide in the atmosphere with the aid of sunlight, then providing them with the means to thrive becomes easy. Organic matter, added back to the soil, builds up a good, friable structure which roots will find easy to penetrate. If you avoid too much walking about on the soil surface, especially when it is wet, you will prevent the particles from becoming compacted together and the structure from becoming spoilt.

Most plants find adequate mineral nutrients from the soil, but in a garden, to improve their

Left: Highlight plants may be quiet in most seasons but will have a period of glory from time to time. Some, like this crab apple (*Malus*), have two major displays: one in spring, when their branches are covered with blossom, and the other in autumn, when the hundreds of small, edible fruits turn to shades of yellow, amber and red.

performance, it will be worth your while to feed them, either with natural organic materials such as rotted manure, or with a proprietary plant food. Whatever their origin, the chemical elements used by all plants are identical.

Care is needed, too, in understanding the precise nature of your garden, and in selecting ideal plants for the specific habitat in which they are expected to grow. Soil type, available light, exposure or degree of shelter, winter and summer temperatures will all combine to make a specific set of conditions to which you must adapt your planting plan, to ensure the best possible displays. This is not difficult to achieve, even

if your garden consists of an unfriendly environment, but it does require thoughtful selection and may need remedial action to improve growing conditions. Later in the book, there is help for specific problem sites (see page 105) and the Great Plant Guide, starting on page 117, will give recommendations for each plant's preferences.

Assuming a workable design and given the vast choice of top-rate plants, it should be possible, regardless of your garden's size, shape, climate and aspect, to enjoy interest, colour, fragrance – and even something to eat – if not every day, at least for a great proportion of the year.

SMALL INFORMAL GARDENS

There are but two kinds of garden: formal and informal. This might appear to over-simplify a complex and diverse art form, but that is what the whole melting pot of garden design boils down to. One way of summarizing the difference is that informal garden design attempts to minimize human influence and to recapture a natural landscape and translate this into a garden setting, while formal gardens have symmetry and order imposed on them which are clearly man-made. We will consider formal gardening in the next chapter (page 37), but here we look at how even the tiniest of informal gardens can be made 'great', not only through design but also by the creative use of plants.

In imitating nature, informal garden layouts make extensive use of natural lines and contours such as the wide, sweeping curve made by a river. While a tiny garden hardly presents opportunities for making huge, lazy S-bends, it is important to keep your lines as bold, as broad and as sweeping as possible, and to avoid fussiness, cramped corners and strange bulges. A large, single curve is graceful at the front of a border, but a small, twisting bend could look more like a wobble than an intentional statement.

In reality, of course, most garden design contains both formal and informal elements. Indeed, one of the strengths of the twentieth-century English garden is that happy marriage between a formal, geometric layout and the informal, naturalistic planting which it contains. Thus, a traditional terrace, perhaps built in mellowed, natural paving stone – possibly even edged with balustrading or a formal wall – might have the harshness of its edges softened by relaxed planting, where shrubs and herbaceous species are allowed to spill over onto the paving, and where climbing plants have been encouraged to scramble over walls and other vertical structures.

Above: This relaxed companion planting of border pinks (*Dianthus*) and lady's mantle (*Alchemilla mollis*) is perfect for the front of an informal border.

Opposite: Walls festooned with climbers, curved beds surrounding a lawn and clusters of pots masking the edges create the essence of informal style and planting in this small town garden. The dramatic tall, black-glazed container forming a focal point on the terrace houses a *Heuchera micrantha* var. *diversifolia* 'Palace Purple'.

Above: Informal borders rely on naturalistic planting and soft, rounded shapes. In this cheerful display for a well-lit but rather dry border, the two spurges (*Euphorbia characias* to the right and *E. polychroma*, left) make a long-lasting gold to green show, set off well by golden-yellow alpine wallflowers, with *Achillea* and Jerusalem sage to follow. Purple honesty (*Lunaria annua*) and a white-flowered *Malus* make a gently colourful background.

INFORMAL DESIGNS

The rules of having a strong, deliberate outline apply to informal as much as to formal gardens and, since an informal garden represents a close imitation of nature, it is likely that plants themselves will provide much of the structural profile. Evergreens like holly, yew and cypress – or, in a very small space, the more diminutive dwarf conifers and low-growing laurels – make fine outline plants, fresh in winter and shapely as summer backgrounds. When arranging the outline, these need to be grouped for optimum effect, rather than being scattered randomly within a more general planting, but always, in an informal setting, the arrangement would imitate a natural landscape.

It is important that structural plants have other advantages, besides being shapely in outline. If using hollies, for example, be sure to select both female and male clones, to ensure a good crop of winter berries. The distinctive *Ilex aquifolium* 'Ferox Argentea' is an excellent male clone, with quietly variegated foliage and prickles over the surface of its leaves, as well as along their margins. Planting this to contrast with the female *I. a.* 'Pyramidalis' will guarantee you two shapely trees and a splendid winter show.

It is important to set off such evergreens, not only with trees that give a good summer and spring contrast – cherries, perhaps, or if room is more limited, lower growing maples – but also with those that provide handsome winter branches and twigs. These skeleton plants create shade and, with careful siting, will provide both a warm, well-lit side and a darker cooler one. The understorey for these outline groups will, of course, be naturalistic but the choice and style of plants will depend on your personal tastes and on the mood you wish to create. (We will return to planting flair when looking at specific locations, later in the chapter.) At this stage we have developed, with our tree and shrub mix, a structure as solid and tangible as a building or a wall, but one that alters from week to week, running through a series of subtle changes in hue, shape and texture through the year. It is also a structure that will grow and therefore need adjusting by removing some trees or shrubs at a future date.

In the informal, as in any garden, it is important to take stock of existing features – buildings, mature trees, walls and so on – and to blend the planting in with them so they make happy companions. Walls and buildings need furnishing, but the choice of plants calls for careful thought. Think whether the flowers or foliage on your climbers will harmonize with the colour of the building material. The reds of some roses, for example, could clash with red brick, but may contrast magnificently with grey stone or white clapboard.

Below: In shady conditions, bright variegation helps to lighten the display. The white-edged foliage of *Cornus alba* is echoed in the foreground by the pure white blooms of *Viola cornuta* 'Alba', an albino Jacob's ladder (*Polemonium caeruleum* 'Album') and the pale grass (*Holcus mollis* 'Variegata').

OUTLINE PLANTS FOR TINY GARDENS

Outline plays as central a role in a really tiny garden as in one on any other scale, but it is even more important, where space is severely restricted, to be ruthlessly selective about your choice of plants. Here are some good, diminutive outline plants for the miniature landscape:

EVERGREEN

Daphne tangutica, D. collina Both have glossy foliage and fragrant pink flowers, mainly in spring but sporadically all summer.
Genista hispanica Spanish gorse, spiny and dome-shaped.
Hebe albicans Good foliage and flower.
Juniperus depressa Forms tiny spires.
***Juniperus communis* 'Hibernica'** Taller spires.
***Picea abies* 'Nidiformis', *Pinus pumila* 'Glauca'** Two tiny conifers.
***Santolina rosmarinifolia* 'Primrose Gem'** Emerald green, can be clipped back tidily; good yellow blooms.

DECIDUOUS

***Potentilla fruticosa* 'Daydawn'** (salmon) and **'Elizabeth'** (yellow) Can be clipped to size.
Prunus tenella Dwarf almond with pink spring blossom.
Prunus cistena Tiny purple-leaved plum.
Salix lanata A small, woolly willow with silver foliage and gnarled winter twigs; pretty when offset by dark evergreens.
Dwarf fruit trees

SPIKY FOLIAGE

***Phormium* 'Bronze Baby'** A dwarf New Zealand flax.
Yucca filamentosa Neatest of the yuccas, with flower spikes less than 1m (3ft).

CLASSIC MIXED BORDER IN SUN

For our first real-garden situation, we will look at a bed bordering a lawn, which is approximately two metres (6½ft) wide, allowing for curves. We will assume reasonable soil, neutral to alkaline, which does not dry out disastrously in summer but which drains reasonably freely in wet winters. With the outline planting at the back of the border, the aim is to create a backdrop and to afford shelter – as well as a little summer shade – to the plants.

The outline planting can be relaxed, with the largest trees allowed to grow relatively high. The aim is for a bright spring display, followed by a quiet early summer. Roses and herbaceous perennials star in the midsummer peak, followed by such choice perennials as asters. Instinct might dictate that the highest point is in the centre, but in a long border an alternative is to have two tall areas, each with a tree at its centre, at either end, with the height reducing towards the middle – rather like soldiers on parade – to create a bold crescent shape.

One of the highest trees could be either a crab apple or a cherry. *Malus* 'Hillieri' is a fine choice for pink-backed spring blossom, but *M.* 'John Downie' is prettier in autumn, when the scarlet and canary yellow fruits form. Among cherries, one of the finest choices is *Prunus sargentii*, not only for the beauty of its dark pink blossom in spring, but for the superb autumn display when the foliage turns to shades of crimson, scarlet and russet orange. To assist with the autumn display, you might include the evergreen *Eucryphia* 'Nymansay' for its white, waxy blooms reminiscent of single camellias but on display from the end of summer into early autumn.

To give informal height below the trees, such tall shrub roses as 'Nevada' (cream) or 'Marguerite Hilling' (pink) provide a flowing, rounded outline, ultimately reaching a couple of metres (6½ft), and smothered in early-summer blooms which look like garlands. The open nature of the shrub roses will need setting off with some solid, leafy material, preferably evergreen and with a contrasting texture. *Elaeagnus ebbingei* goes well here, especially the variety 'Limelight' with its gentle variegations of yellow-green and dark green foliage. A viburnum will give a splash of winter colour; near the *Elaeagnus* 'Limelight', try *V. sargentii* 'Onondaga' whose early-summer, off-white lacecap flowers are set off by superbly bronzed young foliage.

As for the run of understorey plants, the choice is almost unlimited. More roses will be useful to beef up the summer show: among the older varieties, *Rosa gallica* 'Versicolor' has wonderfully striped flowers in deep and pale pink, on plants that seldom exceed a metre (3ft) in height. Sadly, this rose flowers only once, but further blooms could come from one of the best of the China roses, 'Perle d'Or', whose pointed salmon-pink buds are produced in generous waves all through the growing season and deep into autumn, or the similarly shaped, more rosy pink 'Cécile Brunner'.

These shrubs can be underplanted with perennials which will gradually cover the soil and fill the gaps, until the whole border is green and flourishing. Cranesbills such as *Geranium endressii* or the beautiful Asian *G. clarkei* – my favourite is the pale form, 'Kashmir White' – make a gently coloured backing to the brighter, more positively coloured penstemons. The smaller the leaves, with herbaceous penstemons, the hardier the plants seem to be. Although big hybrids of *P. gloxinioides* such as the lavender-blue 'Alice Hindley' make a grander splash, they are less likely to survive frost than narrow-flowered varieties such as the pale pink 'Evelyn'.

The autumn climax can be heightened with a collection of perennial asters. These blend their blues, mauves, pinks and purples warmly with the changing colour of the autumn foliage and on sharp mornings, in the soft, misty light, the effect can be ravishing.

Right: Planting in an informal garden can be as exuberant as you like but there should be a scheme to link the plants together. The colours in this seemingly muddled jumble of flowers and leaves are in fact thoughtfully teamed. The pink-backed petals of *Lilium regale* correspond with the dark foliage of *Berberis thunbergii* 'Rose Glow' and link with the brighter pink of the lavatera. The 'Monte Rosa' lily (right) makes a happy companion to the dark-flowered dahlia, tying all the colours together. Making a quiet but harmonious background is the glaucous-leaved *Rosa glauca* which, in autumn, will carry bright red fruits.

Select disease-resistant species such as *Aster amellus,* *A. lateriflorus, A novae-angliae* and *A.x frikartii.* The crocosmias, especially late kinds such as 'Solfaterre' and 'Emily McKenzie', blend sumptuously with perennial asters, introducing warm shades – orange in the latter and soft amber in the former – set off by bronze-tinged leaves.

All that remains, for this informal border, is a selection of highlight plants. Winter can be brightened with some Christmas roses (*Helleborus niger);* 'Potter's Wheel' boasts large, well-shaped, waxy white flowers from mid-winter until mid-spring. For spring highlights, the later, rosy theme could be anticipated with a generous sprinkling of pink tulips, dotted about in groups rather than massed in one area. Try the lovely Viridiflora variety, 'Greenland', for early bloom, with its pink petals suffused with green, followed later by the old-fashioned cottage tulip 'Clara Butt'. Alliums make a splash in later spring, looking wonderful with the first of the peonies. Most are in the mauve or purple range, the strongest colours coming from *A. aflatunense* and the closely related garden clone, 'Purple Sensation', but a better plant for colonizing a sunny border is *A. christophii,* not only for its large, silvery-mauve globe flowers, but also for the drama of its maturing seedheads.

A WOODLAND GARDEN

Above: Foliage plays a more important role than flowers in this shaded garden. Ferns, bergenia, euphorbia and Solomon's seal (*Polygonatum* x *hybridum*) provide contrasting foliage shapes and colours. The white flowers of the mophead hydrangea furnish a bright highlight against the green background.

The idea of developing one's garden into a natural woodland glade is highly romantic but the reality is that in most small gardens the 'woodland' sections occupy a relatively dark corner. You may have an area shaded by a building, making for constant, dense shade. Perhaps tall trees in or near your garden throw dense shade in summer but in winter and spring, before the leaves emerge, admit enough light for a wider choice of spring-flowering plants. Shade in a garden often brings associated problems of dry soil, caused by excessive shelter from rain – a problem dealt with in a later chapter (page 109). But in a more favoured shady site you might have dappled shade and reasonably moist, more or less neutral soil.

The most likely site for a woodland theme, in a small garden, is under a specimen tree. In the wild, most soil beneath trees is rich in organic material, consisting almost entirely of fallen leaves, in varying stages of decay, rotting down to add to the thickening layer of leafmould. But in a garden, for the sake of tidiness and good management, fallen foliage is usually raked up and, hopefully, composted for later use. It is important to build up the humus level beneath the tree(s) by returning composted leaves to the surface, or by chopping or shredding plant material and spreading it back straight away.

The flowering season begins early in a well planted woodland garden, with winter aconites (*Eranthis hyemalis*) and the first snowdrops beginning to appear soon after the shortest day. In midwinter these small flowers bring intense delight. Snowdrops are happy almost anywhere and, for enthusiasts, there are hundreds of different kinds. Among wild species, the common snowdrop (*Galanthus nivalis*) is the most frequently grown, but a larger cousin from the Crimea, *G. elwesii*, blooms earlier, with stems that reach up to 25cm (10in) and flowers over 2.5cm (1in) long. Among cultivars, one of the largest is the huge, scented *G. nivalis* 'Sam Arnott' and one of the most dramatic, close-to, is the double 'Ophelia' whose flower centres make tightly packed green rosettes.

To follow these early treasures, the choice of shade-loving spring plants is almost unlimited. This is the brightest season, before foliage emerges on the trees to shade the ground. The traditional spring plants – primroses, violets, wood anemones and, later, bluebells – can be more tricky to establish than those which are used to drier conditions, later in the year. To help them thrive, it will be essential to improve their soil with moisture-retentive mulches or leafmould. Tougher subjects than these spring gems, but no less

beautiful, are the oriental hellebores, which link winter with spring, and such North American natives as epimediums, erythroniums and false Solomon's seal (*Smilacina racemosa*). Epimedium is a tough genus which has the advantage of decorative foliage, in most of its species, which changes colour through the year. *Epimedium rubrum*, for example, as well as producing cherry-red blooms in spring, develops a canopy of leaves, held on wiry stems, which run through a fascinating sequence of changes.

By the time summer arrives, the environment has changed so much, under the trees, that a new set of conditions will apply. Plants which flowered in spring will be rushing to produce seed, before too much of the light has disappeared, and those that flower in summer will be few and far between. Your main display may become limited to the fringes of the woodland garden, the areas where a beam or two of sunshine can allow the common foxglove (*Digitalis purpurea*) to bloom, perhaps in the company of the woodland cranesbill (*Geranium sylvaticum*). For high summer, the woodland garden is likely to become a quiet area, with little to excite the senses. If you plant baneberry (*Actaea rubra*), the conspicuous bright red berries will ripen soon after the longest day, giving a small taste of the berry season to come.

Autumn can be like a second spring, with a return of bright, clean colours, mainly from bulbous or tuberous plants. The hardy cyclamen species are a perfect choice, even for the smallest garden, because they combine so many excellent characteristics. Easiest and best known is the frost-hardy *C. hederifolium* which flowers in late summer and continues throughout autumn. The first blooms, in shades of pink or a clean white, precede the foliage but, later, leaves which are richly marbled in silver and grey develop and last right through the darkest months, when they make charming companions to the late winter-blooming *C. coum* and such spring beauties as primroses or *Anemone nemorosa*.

Left: Creating a woodland mood here are plants from different continents. The European wood anemone (*Anemone nemorosa*) produces a carpet of lacy foliage topped with frail white blooms in early spring. It makes a perfect teammate for the North American species, *Erythronium revolutum*, whose handsomely veined foliage precedes the elegant, swept-back pink flowers.

A GRAVEL GARDEN

Below: Hot conditions and good drainage suit most artemisias, whose decorative silver foliage is useful for making bold contrasts. Here, the frost-tender *A. stelleriana* sets off the bronze leaves of sedum. The mauve flowers belong to *Tulbaghia violacea*.

One tends to think of plants growing in borders or beds, but another way of creating a delightful and interesting informal garden is to use gravel as a surface, not merely for the pathways but as a habitat in which to develop a planting scheme. The advantages of coarse grit, or pea-size gravel, are considerable, not only as a permanent mulch but, for some plants, even as a growing medium. Gravel makes a continuous surface, combining growing areas with pathways and opening up the whole concept of the design layout. When carefully chosen to suit the colours and textures of its surroundings, it can in fact make a more attractive setting, especially for small plants, than border soil. A gravel surface also drains well, suiting plants which dislike wet feet, especially in winter, and moisture is conserved below a gravel mulch.

A gravel garden looks most realistic in an informal setting, when it has been arranged to imitate nature most closely. In the wild, this is likely to be either a mountainous scree, a lake or marine foreshore, or a river bed. Some of the most naturalistic designs use alluvial gravel of different sizes in swirls, lines and eddies which imitate the natural variations found in a river bed. Large features – boulders, perhaps, groups of larger shrubs or such man-made artefacts as well-heads, water pumps or statuary – will give the design shape and focus.

In a gravel garden of my own, I use two large lumps of tufa – porous natural limestone – as a focal point. These are about a metre (3ft 3in) across and planted with cushion saxifrages and small primulas. The rectangular gravel area, measuring about 4 metres (13ft) by 9 metres (30ft), is divided by a serpentine path marked out with paving stones, set into the gravel at stepping intervals. Below the pebbles the soil is variable – limestone rubble in some parts, heavyish alkaline clay in others. On either side of the path, the mainstream planting is shared between dwarf bearded irises for the early spring display, followed by a collection of helianthemums whose colours range through reds, orange, pale yellow and soft pink. Many are named cultivars, such as 'Raspberry Ripple' or 'Wisley Primrose' and the fiery red, double-flowered 'Mrs Earle', but others are seedlings that have cropped up as volunteers in the gravel and been allowed to stay.

My anchor shrub is the Spanish gorse (*Genista hispanica*), whose dome shape has now embraced the low wall that divides the terrace from the driveway, invading far too much space, but too lovely to destroy.

Several wild or semi-wild oreganos thrive in this sunny spot, particularly the purple-flowered *O. laevigatum* and its lower-growing relative, *O. rotundifolium* whose little hop-like blossoms in pale green are enchanting throughout the summer. Among these scramble wild thymes (*Thymus vulgaris*), not so much for their flower colours, but for the usefulness of their evergreen foliage. Low-growing, variegated forms are best for winter colour, particularly the varieties 'Bertram Anderson' or 'Anderson's Gold', both of which have yellow foliage, and the bottle green, cream-flecked 'Doone Valley' whose leaves develop little russet highlights in cold weather.

Extending the seasons on such a gravel garden is simple. Bulbs are indispensable, partly because their contribution is large in relation to the space they occupy and also because they disappear reasonably quickly after their season is over. Little bulbs from arid regions – South African ixias and chincherinchees (*Ornithogalum thyrsoides*), perhaps, or Mediterranean anemones, bulbous irises and the more drought-resistant fritillaries, such as *Fritillaria gussichiae* – all make useful contributions, as do *Ornithogalum nutans* and the extraordinary black and green-flowered iris from Greece, *Hermodactylus tuberosus*. In mild conditions, many of these bulbs will seed copiously among the gravel, bulking up numbers so freely that you almost have to hoe out the surplus!

Where soil below the gravel is reasonably fertile and moisture-retentive, the choice of plants widens to include lusher, bolder species. The smaller cranesbills love to scramble among the stones and one of the prettiest of these is the bloody cranesbill (*Geranium sanguineum*) but in its pale sub-species, *G. s. striatum*. Study an individual bloom and you will notice how the soft pink is scored with darker pencil lines. And *G. dalmaticum* makes a shorter-lasting, but equally effective display, particularly in its white and very pale pink forms. The hybrid *G.* x *cantabrigiense* 'Biokovo' has flowers in the palest shade of pink – almost white

– held above rounded, sweetly aromatic foliage in early summer. Later, the foliage takes on autumnal hues but is practically evergreen, the old leaves persisting until the new growth takes over in spring. Blue flowers contrast prettily with reddening leaves in autumn and these can be provided by *Ceratostigma plumbaginoides*, a plant whose own foliage turns reddish for autumn, making a gorgeous contrast with the deep azure of the bloom produced through late summer and autumn.

For winter glory in gravel, besides such bulbs as crocuses and the tiny reticulata irises already mentioned, you could try the dwarf *Forsythia viridissima* 'Bronxensis' which forms stiff, twiggy shrublets smothered in mid-yellow blooms in late winter, or such low, tidy evergreens as daphnes (for example, *D. tangutica*) or, in semi-shade, sweet smelling sarcococcas. All these will link the seasons, ensuring a pleasing picture through the year.

Above: Grey-leaved plants often associate well with gravel. The foliage of the blue spruce (*Picea pungens* 'Prostrata') here becomes the central focus of a glaucous colour theme. A grey-leaved dwarf willow (*Salix helvetica*) and the variegated *Iris pallida* ring the changes in form and texture. The white blossoms in the background are those of *Viburnum plicatum*.

31

A GARDEN FOR WILDLIFE

Gardeners the world over are becoming increasingly aware of environmental issues and many see their gardens as having great potential for fostering wildlife (the beneficial species, that is). In fact, gardens in general tend to be good havens for a great many species of birds, small mammals and other vertebrates and, above all, insects. All you need to do, as a supporter of wildlife, is to make small adjustments to accommodate a richer variety of species.

The most important needs for wildlife are food sources, somewhere to reproduce, and somewhere to live. Your main objective is to provide cover – that is, a series of havens or refuges where the species can hide. A pond is an obvious development (covered in a later chapter, page 71), but long, thick vegetation, not only near the pond but in other quiet corners, will help considerably. Permanent climbers or wall plants provide good cover, especially evergreens like English ivy (*Hedera*) – one of the best refuges for many species of over-wintering insect – and a varied but fairly permanent ground cover helps to enhance the habitat.

Tidiness is acceptable – essential even, in a small garden – but excessive grooming is unhelpful, not only to wildlife but it can ruin the relaxed feel of an informal planting. Allowing perennials, for instance, to remain untrimmed throughout autumn not only feeds seed-eating birds but also provides shelter. In an informal border, if the perennials are all in good health as they decline gently into dormancy, they can look ravishing with the development of autumn colours. If you select such plants as sedums, centaureas, *Phlomis russeliana* and *Euphorbia palustris*, the autumn outline and colours of the dying leaves can be as beautiful as the summer climax of fresh growth.

Food supplies for wildlife come either directly from your plants, or from the species that live on the plants. Berries and fruits help to make a rich display in autumn and to feed a great many birds. But insects and other invertebrates feed song birds, so it is important to think carefully before using insecticide sprays. In most cases, they are unnecessary in a well-managed garden. If aphids are a problem on roses, judicious use of control measures will not threaten wild birds or other insect species either.

THE WILDLIFE-FRIENDLY BORDER

Good design principles still apply, but a little more care is needed in selecting as many species as possible that will be of benefit to wildlife, as well as meeting the exacting demands of being 'great plants'. A fruit tree – a good self-pollinating apple, perhaps, such as a Bramley – might make a fine anchor point. Whatever fruits you do not harvest can feed birds and squirrels for some time. Alternatively, try one of the hawthorns – select a single-flowered, fruit-bearing variety or a true species such as the Afghanistan native, *Crataegus tanacetifolia*. Holly is great for berries and can be adapted to take on almost any shape: *Ilex aquifolium* is one of the best berrying species (you need male and female plants to obtain fruits) and comes in lovely variegated forms as well as plain green. My favourite is the bright creamy yellow- and green-variegated 'Madame Briot', which produces a good berry crop and whose foliage takes on a bronzy hue in hard winter weather.

For foliage plants, try *Arum italicum* 'Pictum', which has startling red berry stems in autumn and attractive, marbled foliage at other times, looking pretty with primulas in spring and cranesbills (*Geranium* species) in summer. Honesty (*Lunaria annua*), is a good butterfly plant for late spring but the main run of butterfly nectar plants – though not those on which their larvae feed – include lavender, *Sedum spectabile, Verbena bonariensis, Aubrieta* and, most popular of all, *Buddleja davidii*. Winter berries can also come from *Mahonia pinnata*, with its lovely yellow

blooms and handsome evergreen foliage, and from a selection of cotoneasters or pyracanthas.

Dense ground cover, if there happens to be a shady end to this wildlife border, could come from the lesser periwinkle (*Vinca minor*), which has several interesting varieties, with variegated foliage and with both double and single blooms in blue, magenta or white. At the feet of the larger shrubs or wall plants, these will not only offer a generous refuge for all kinds of beasties, but also provide spring colour with their flowers and a cool, foliage effect for later summer.

For a final flourish to your wildlife border, you might install an obelisk to carry a fragrant, berry-bearing honeysuckle, or to encourage one to climb into the principal tree. *Lonicera periclymenum* is a berry-rich species and the clone 'Graham Thomas' flowers profusely in early summer, followed by a long succession of sporadic blooms later, to blend with the red berries. The flower colours are soft yellow, deepening to straw as they age – a supreme wildlife species and a great plant for even the smallest garden.

Above: A glorious miscellany of wild cornfield flowers includes daisies, corn marigold and field poppies. Since most of these species are annual, they will need soil conditions that lend themselves to sowing; dense grass will be less suitable than newly worked soil.

Opposite: This small garden has been made wildlife-friendly by allowing the grass to grow longer than normal for a lawn (though not long enough to be untidy) and by growing largely wild species of plants which will better meet the needs of the local fauna.

A WILDLIFE BORDER

This flower border has lasting interest and beauty while providing a home for many wildlife species. The fallen log shelters insects, which in turn encourage birds into the garden. Plenty of low-growing, mat-forming plants give shelter and an old stump, which is host to a variety of wildlife-friendly climbers, is backed by a buddleja to provide nectar for butterflies. The lawn surrounding the bed is close mown in parts but also has areas of longer grass, studded with daisies and buttercups. Hip-bearing roses, an ornamental blackberry and sweet violets extend the period of interest well beyond the early summer season shown.

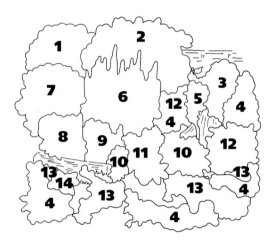

THE PLANTS

1 *Rubus cockburnianus* 'Golden Vale'

2 *Buddleja davidii*

3 *Clematis alpina* 'Ruby'

4 Poppies, including *Papaver rhoeas*

5 *Lonicera peridymenum*

6 *Digitalis purpurea*

7 *Rosa moyesii* 'Scarlet Fire'

8 *Ajuga reptans* 'Braunhertz'

9 *Lamium maculatum* 'White Nancy'

10 *Viola cornuta*

11 *Primula veris*

12 *Centaurea cyanus*

13 *Bellis perennis*

14 *Viola odorata*

SMALL FORMAL GARDENS

While informal gardens are imitations of natural landscapes, formal gardens are clearly to do with the intervention of man and reflect those uniquely human concepts of symmetry, order, geometry, form and style. Strictly formal gardens are in fact more akin to architecture than to nature. Indeed, they are extensions of buildings and other structures which, instead of, or as well as, using building materials such as stone and timber, also deploy living plants – but the plants are permitted to grow only within the strictly preordained proportions of the garden structure. However severe and formal a garden design, it can often be made to accommodate informal planting. The two styles may be opposites – the garden's structure may even be rigid and uncompromising in style – but they dovetail comfortably together in many of the most successful gardens, where geometric shapes and hard edges are softened by naturalistic planting.

Contemporary formal garden design is often closely tied in with the architecture of the house. The line and form the garden takes, particularly in a small space, will lead from doorways and windows, making the garden an extended room, closely related to the interior. Views from the most important windows have a symmetry and, even where corners are turned and different areas are enclosed from the main garden, the pattern of pathways, beds, borders or terraces will almost always link with the main design. This can be very different from informal designs, which might strive for a wide variety of different moods and effects.

Above: In this original approach to garden design, box, clipped into neat globes, is planted symmetrically within a paved area. The evergreen plants ensure year-round freshness, while the artificial layout dictates a strictly formal feel.

Opposite: Formality in a tiny space: low box hedges and brickwork create a formal niche, while bedded hostas provide a contrast in texture and a different shade of greenery. The weeping pear (*Pyrus salicifolia*) and the rose soften the severity of the line without damaging the overall geometric design.

Above: This formal garden uses plants for structure. Apart from the trellis obelisks, paths and seat, the line comes from the low hedge boundaries and the symmetrical repetition of the main plant, honeysuckle.

PLANTING IN A FORMAL DESIGN

Planting schemes for formal gardens should help to enhance their structure. Natural beauty is still present, of course, but the plants are used as materials for composing formal patterns rather than for painting a naturalistic picture. Hedges, one of the most prominent features of formal gardens, are clearly man-made structures (you never see a symmetrical row of shrubs in the wild) and as such comprise part of the layout, yet at the same time they are growing, living plants.

Whether clipped as low border edgings, grown tall to create barriers or used to draw the complicated patterns of knot gardens or small parterres, hedges are as artificial as manufactured structures like pergolas, fences or walls. But just think of the rich variety of shapes, textures and hues that can be achieved with different hedging materials! Rosemary, for example, is quick-growing, aromatic and spiky. Cherry laurel (*Prunus laurocerasus*) grows fast and has smooth, shiny evergreen foliage, contrasting gently with the darker, slow-growing yew (*Taxus baccata*), the classic choice of formal hedge material since Roman times. Dark evergreens make an even more dramatic contrast with beech (*Fagus*) or hornbeam (*Carpinus*), especially in winter when the hornbeam foliage has turned light brown and the beech leaves have assumed their special shade of rich tan.

Hedges on a much smaller scale can be created from lavender, cotton lavender (*Santolina*), low-growing varieties of laurel (like *Prunus laurocerasus* 'Otto Luykens') and, of course, dwarf box (*Buxus sempervirens* 'Suffruticosa'). All can be clipped regularly and, despite considerable age, kept as low as 30cm (12in).

In the formal garden, the shape and position of the plants is critical. So too is the choice and arrangement of colours and, to a lesser extent, of the types of foliage and habit displayed by the plants. But the main planting principles – of outline, understorey and highlights – still apply. The outline plants may be as formal and artificial as pleached trees, topiary or hedging, or may be selected from those plants, such as fastigiate yews or drumstick maples, which are naturally disciplined in shape. The understorey could consist of ground-cover planting, where a small selection of varieties are planted in large numbers, or might have the contrived appearance of a formal bedding display. And highlight plants might be natural specimens, placed in a specific site: a camellia in a container as a vista stop, or a climbing rose grown on a pillar or obelisk.

Below: Complicated hedging patterns, inspired by the large-scale *parterres,* or knot gardens, of earlier centuries, can be scaled down to whatever size is appropriate. A miniaturized knot garden, here using box, thyme and ivy, backed by trellis panels, makes a strong feature in a tiny space.

OUTLINE PLANTS FOR FORMAL STATEMENTS

TOPIARY
Long-term, slow to develop, but superb quality: holly; yew; *Prunus lusitanica*.

Speedy for quick results: ivy or muhlenbeckia, grown on a frame.

Naturally formal: *Juniperus scopulorum* 'Skyrocket'; *J. communis* 'Hibernica'; *Prunus* 'Umineko'.

SIMPLE STATEMENTS
Long-term: wisteria, trained on an obelisk, kept small, or pruned into a small tree; *Sophora japonica* (weeping form); laburnum, trained on a frame.

Speedy: *Salix daphnoides* or *Cornus alba*, pruned as winter pollards.

PILLAR ROSES FOR SMALL GARDENS
Red: 'Danse du Feu'; 'Climbing Alec's Red'; 'Paul's Scarlet'; 'Guinée'.
Grey-pink: 'Ash Wednesday'.
Yellow: 'Mermaid'; 'Golden Showers'; 'Gloire de Dijon'.
Apricot: 'Lady Hillingdon'.
White: 'Climbing Iceberg'; 'Madame Alfred Carrière'.

FORMAL FRONT GARDENS

Front gardens are viewed as much by others as by their owners, but they are seldom viewed for long periods. For that reason, a formal design, whose structure and content can be taken in at a single glance, or whose layout is so interesting that it causes people to slow down as they pass, is likely to be more rewarding than a wild or informal planting which, at certain times of the year, can look rather a mess.

A FORMAL FRONT GARDEN WITH PERMANENT PLANTING

Small front gardens often lend themselves to a formal treatment and certain aspects of historic gardening continue to be appealing today. For example, the concept of arranging small beds, often lozenge-shaped, on either side of a central path to the door of the house would have been almost as commonplace in Roman times as it is now. If such beds were furnished with permanent ground cover, if there were low hedges of myrtle with, perhaps, a pomegranate tree in the centre of each, the Roman feel would be authentic. On its own, this design would be somewhat sterile but, enriched with more imaginative planting and

Right: Planting schemes for formal gardens should help to enhance the garden's structure. Natural beauty is still present, of course, but the plants are used as materials for composing formal patterns, rather than for painting a natural picture.

with a slightly more interesting arrangement of beds – perhaps using a mix of gravel and old stone paving – and the addition of a distinctive, theftproof artefact, you could have the makings of a front garden that provides pleasure and excitement through the seasons.

THE OUTLINE Bordering hedges provide the line and form of a design but they also contribute much during winter, when colour and lushness are at a low ebb. Hedge plants which flower, or bear berries, are particularly useful. Myrtle has the bonus of sweetly aromatic foliage, but needs a gentle climate; lavender is hardier, and provides rich colour in summer; many of the cotoneasters and pyracanthas are indestructible, but box keeps its shape better than any of them and needs but one annual clipping.

Planting hedges in a knot style, along Elizabethan lines, sounds complicated but is easier than you might imagine and can be relatively quick to establish. Box hedging is extremely costly, if you plan to buy your plants, but box can be propagated by breaking off branches or small twigs and sticking them into the ground, where they should root within months. The drawback is the time they can take to develop: they sometimes sulk for a year before even starting to grow, and the best kinds for dwarf hedging, such as *Buxus sempervirens* 'Suffruticosa' develop even more slowly.

THE INFILL Simplified versions of traditional knot patterns are effective and positively beg to be interplanted with interesting perennials. Where they create small enclosures, these can be filled with spreading plants. It is best to choose uniform varieties and select those which contribute contrasting foliage colour as well as flower. Thus the silver, silky filigree artemisias, such as *A.* 'Lambrook Silver' or the grey-green *A. pontica*, or the white felty foliage of *Stachys olympica* make a strong contrast with dark green box. In shade – and a good many front gardens are shaded – hostas or the dark-leaved forms of bugle (*Ajuga reptans*) are even

more effective. Artemisias can be clipped back to create uniformity of size but hostas cannot, so select hosta varieties that will not overshadow the hedging or the plants inside the knot. Lily-of-the-valley (*Convallaria majalis*) is even more valuable ground cover for shade than are hostas, since its foliage is fresher for longer and its blooms are intensely scented.

If a knot garden is too fussy for your taste, the principle of using low hedging is still sound in a formal garden. The discipline they impose on the planting is useful in a restricted space, giving form but keeping up the quotient of greenery.

HIGHLIGHTS In a formal front garden of this kind, highlight plants are still needed to provide joyful surprises through the seasons. Bulbs are, as ever, great contributors, especially tulips, since they are good-natured enough to die down quite quickly, or can be lifted to another part of the garden after flowering, without harm. It is always important to think of scale and to select medium or dwarf plants in restricted spaces, but tulips last for such a short time that it might be more fun to splash out on some outsize colour. Huge, ruffled parrot tulips or the stately, lily-flowered kinds could positively tower over the small

Above: This front garden displays an alluring marriage of formal layout in a largely rustic setting. The thatched roof, front door and stacked logs are romantically informal but the beds, squared with low box hedges, bring a more solid, year-round structure to the garden and allow for changing planting within.

41

Above: Brick paths, gravel and topiary mark out the layout of the formal rose garden. The central area features modern hybrid roses, underplanted with foliage plants such as lavender, *Stachys olympica* and lady's mantle.

Opposite: In this formal cruciform design, two paths intersect; a willow-leaved pear (*Pyrus salicifolia*) becomes a focal point at the centre. Within the stepped, clipped hedges the planting is relaxed, with old-fashioned roses and companion plants.

hedges, making a magnificent display. And there is no better idea than to have them burst forth from a mist of autumn-planted forget-me-not blooms (*Myosotis*).

Later, such tall alliums as *A. aflatunense* or *A. giganteum* are as spectacular as tulips, and after them, in high summer, the tall white *Galtonia candicans* or the less coarse forms of gladiolus can continue the bulb theme. Bearded flag irises may be short-lived in bloom but they have pleasant, sword-like foliage and tolerate a summer baking so, in a bright front garden, vivid-coloured varieties can be used to excellent effect for early summer. *Iris germanica* 'Wabash' has bright purple-blue and stark white flowers, 'Edward of Windsor' is soft apricot in colour and 'Frost and Flame' is one of the most exciting, its stark white petals making an icy contrast with the scarlet orange of its beard.

In winter, when every garden tends to rely on structure and shape, formal designs are often at their absolute best. Conifers, evergreens, hedges and even topiary, which may have taken a back seat during summer's excesses, all combine to present a structure which is pleasing to look at. If any more is needed in a well designed formal garden, it is a careful selection of winter highlights to relieve any monotony. A hellebore, a small group of snowdrops (*Galanthus*), winter jasmine (*J. nudiflorum*) on a wall – the single splash of delight is all you need to be enticed outdoors on a cold day. Even in the formal structural planting, evergreen hedges can be punctuated with flowering daphnes, many of which are also evergreen, or containers with winter foliage compositions (for ideas, see page 99).

A FORMAL ROSE GARDEN

Modern shrub roses lend themselves to symmetrical, geometric beds and, since roses need much personal attention – pruning, spraying, feeding and so on – a formal rose garden facilitates their practical care.

Where mixed roses are grown, it is less easy to create a formal effect but using uniform companion plants can help to pull the design together. Blues, especially the soft, smoky blues of catmint, lavender, perovskia or many of the cranesbills tie roses together successfully without shouting at their colours. *Nepeta* 'Six Hills Giant', for instance, looks as handsome with the yellow hues of such roses as 'Peace' or 'Graham Thomas' as with the burning tones of 'Alec's Red' or the gentler, shell pink or salmon of 'Blessings' or 'Just Joey', making a fine plant for furnishing their bases.

Wonderful though they may be for six months, roses can look horrible for the rest of the year, pruned back to stumps with no outline and no winter foliage. Companion plants, therefore, need not only to associate well with roses during the growing season, but also to provide some compensation for their winter gloom. Evergreen foliage is useful here, which is why a bordering hedge of lavender or box always works well and the bold, leathery foliage of *Bergenia cordifolia* also helps to set off the rose blooms in summer, especially if you use the white-flowered form, 'Silberlicht'.

COLOUR IN A FORMAL SCHEME

With any garden, one uses colours to paint pictures, but in a formal one, where the cultivation is less natural and the dimensions and arrangements are more distinctly artificial, colour can be used in far more contrived ways. Plants become materials with which to create specific colour effects, especially when these are grouped or massed together.

It is important to consider colour first in almost abstract terms, then to apply these to the planting. The choice of colour combinations depends on personal preferences, of course, and it is not pertinent for garden writers to pontificate – but certain rules, if observed, do tend to give better results. In a formal planting, plain colours invariably look better than mixtures, and it is worth thinking carefully about hues that seem to work well together before you begin selecting plants. In this respect, planning flower and foliage colours is no different from planning the decor of a room: you might begin with the vaguest ideas about colours but these gradually become translated into specific wallpapers, paints, carpet, curtains and so on. Outdoors, you might develop general ideas about the colour scheme you want – and this will often be influenced either by what is growing there permanently or by the colour of the house. Gradually, your colour plans take shape and get translated into a shortlist of actual plant species and varieties.

In a restricted space, you must plan your colour schemes especially carefully, particularly if more than a single scheme will be visible at once. This presents a challenge but, even in a tiny area, you can arrange your planting so that there are gentle colour transitions from one spot to another. Some examples of successful colour combinations are given in the box (right), with suggestions for plants that will provide them.

CREATING A PERIOD FLAVOUR

If you wish your formal garden to have a period feel, it is worth studying the planting plans of the Victorians, those masters of bedding schemes. The effect of their summer schemes is very different from the colour and spectacle of some of today's bedding displays, in which the purpose seems to be to plant to excess, and where vivid flower colours – the orange of marigolds, the red of salvias, the mixed hues of petunias, busy lizzies and pelargoniums – blot out all traces of restful greens. The Victorians' schemes were no less dramatic but usually more carefully considered, with clever combinations of foliage, subtle colour blends and careful 'staging' of plants, with regard to their heights, dimensions and special characteristics.

In a tiny garden, impact is important but so is the nature of the planting composition. Colour, used with caution, is likely to make a brighter, bolder statement than indiscriminate planting. Bear in mind that foliage counts for as much as bloom, if not more: a useful exercise is to consider the foliage effect first,

Below: Foliage plants are woven here to create a colourful living carpet, with contrasting colours and differing textures. Regular clipping is needed to keep a formal bedding scheme looking fresh and neat. Box and cotton lavender require only a single annual cut, but the purple-leaved sage needs several treatments a season.

Purple and gold: *Physocarpus opulifolius* 'Dart's Gold' with *Cotinus* 'Grace'.

Green with yellow and white: most variegated foliage with daffodils; green nicotiana with yellow African marigolds; snowdrops and winter aconites; *Ornithogalum nutans* with golden creeping jenny (*Lysimachia nummularia* 'Aurea').

Red with yellow: salvias with rudbeckia.

Red with green flowers: *Nicotiana langsdorffii* with *Penstemon* 'Firebird'; *Alstroemeria psittacina* on its own.

Pink and blue: larkspurs, cornflowers and *Clematis macropetala* come in both colours; *Pulmonaria saccharata* has pink and blue flowers on the same plant; campanulas, cranesbills, perennial asters.

Yellow and black: *Viola* 'Bowles Black' planted with *V.* 'Jackanapes'.

Silver and pink: most species of dianthus, especially 'Cheddar Pink', or most border pinks; pink petunias with *Senecio* 'Silver Dust' or *S. viravira*.

Apricot and maroon: *Rosa* 'Lady Hillingdon' with *Cosmos atrosanguineus*; *Digitalis* 'Sutton's Apricot' with *Paeonia delavayi*.

Purple or mauve with cream or lemon: *Tulipa* 'Maytime' with cream wallflowers; *Erysimum* 'Chelsea Jacket' with cream tulips; purple heliotrope with the cream African marigold, 'Vanilla Ice'.

Orange and blue: Blue wallflowers with marigolds (*Calendula*); orange dahlias or *Tithonia rotundifolia* with *Anchusa*; tulip 'Prinses Irene' with forget-me-nots (*Myosotis*).

then dream up some colours that will go with the leaves. Silvery foliage, for example, is so often used as a backing for pink schemes that the colour combination has become something of a cliché; but, if you consider the effect that silver and bronze can have, when united, and then think of how flowers in maroon, crimson or apricot would harmonize with these, especially if they were dotted or placed sparingly among the foliage, you have the makings of a gentler scheme. The choice of plants could be as simple as you like. Pale orange *Calendula* could be planted among *Amaranthus* and *Senecio* 'Silver Dust'. Or how about a single bed, packed with the white, felty foliage of *Artemisia ludoviciana*, among which you have dotted *Lobelia cardinalis*, as much for the contrast of its deep purple foliage as for the startling scarlet blooms? The dahlia 'Bishop of Llandaff' would have a similar effect.

Above: In formal planting, colour is used as a painter might use it, spreading strong brush strokes for an intense impact and stippling for a softer effect. Vivid blue delphiniums here combine with *Geranium magnificum*, whose smaller flowers are a more purple-hued blue, and contrast with the golden-leaved marjoram (*Origanum vulgare* 'Aureum').

A FORMAL FRONT GARDEN

Symmetry rules in this formal front garden, seen here in late summer. The rectangular area separating the house from the street has been divided into two enclosed squares with a central path to the front door. The square beds contain a mixture of permanent planting (*Santolina neapolitana*) and temporary bedding (*Nicotiana*). At a glance, the colour impact is assertive but not garish, with pink, silver and green predominating in the foreground. The colour scheme is reflected more strongly in the background, where the narrow border against the wall of the house displays harder reds, backed with silver foliage and contrasted with white and a little blue. Clematis and climbing roses are planted against the house.

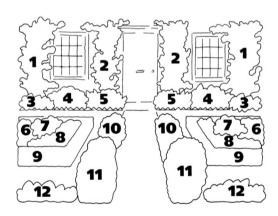

THE PLANTS

1 *Rosa* 'Albéric Barbier'

2 *Clematis* 'Madame Julia Correvon'

3 *Bergenia* 'Silberlicht'

4 *Anaphalis margaritacea*

5 *Penstemon* 'Schoenholzeri'

6 *Santolina neapolitana*

7 *Aeonium arboreum*

   'Arnold Schwarzkopff'

8 *Nicotiana* 'Domino Salmon'

9 *Buxus sempervirens*

10 *Lavandula angustifolia*

11 *Rosmarinus officinalis*

12 *Bergenia cordifolia* 'Purpurea'

SMALL COTTAGE GARDENS

The idea of the cottage garden is based more on romantic notions than on hard facts. In reality, cottage gardens were used for subsistence rather than for pleasure in a countryside where evidence of poverty was as much part of the landscape as were trees and pastures. The cottagers' small incomes came from the land and their habitation was crude and strictly functional. You would be as likely to find chickens and a pig in the garden, as vegetables, and the space for such unnecessary components as flowers and ornamental plants would be very limited indeed. It was not until the nineteenth-century rural reforms of such philanthropists as John Claudius Loudon, who tried to improve the lot of the rural poor by persuading the gentry to start cottage improvement schemes, that cottages on the great landowners' estates began to be seen as making a decorative contribution to the countryside.

Loudon, who also designed many of London's squares, bringing fragments of the countryside into the growing city, gave advice on the architecture of the cottages and recommended minimum dimensions for cottagers' gardens. Thus, the romantic idea began to grow. In nineteenth-century English literature, we find cottagers creating pretty gardens: in George Eliot's *Silas Marner*, for example, Marner's adopted daughter plants flowers outside his dwelling and Thomas Hardy, writing in the late nineteenth century about former times, describes gardens attached to cottages. As an increasing number of tenants became home owners, the concept of the cottage garden evolved into a particular style whose popularity has ebbed and flowed, with shifting tastes and patterns, ever since.

Above: The essence of cottage-style plants: a McKanna Hybrid columbine (*Aquilegia*) grows among the pungent-smelling, ferny foliage and pink flowers of the wild European cranesbill (*Geranium robertianum*).

Opposite: The classic cottage garden border is rich with different colours and flower shapes but maintains harmony by a careful choice of companion plants. Tall red hot pokers (*Kniphofia*) and bellflowers (*Campanula persicifolia*) make strong upright features, backed by a mass of smaller, lower-growing blooms including pot marigolds and anthemis.

49

COTTAGE-GARDEN STYLE

For our purposes, cottage-garden style can be defined, in its simplest form, as random planting within a confined space. It is necessarily a marriage of formal and informal design – formal only in the need to contain planting within bounds by using pathways, building and the boundaries of the plot; informal because the planting is random at best, ramshackle at worst. Whether rural or urban, a cottage garden has seductive charm: the jumble of flowers, bright colours, such romantic artefacts as beehives or antique cloches, roses round the door and even a creaky wicket gate all help to create cottage style.

The most important ingredient of any cottage garden is the planting. The design might be – and often is – as basic a layout as twin plots, divided by a central path, leading to a door. This in itself does not constitute a cottage garden but, if planted with a rich miscellany of species to provide several small areas of colour, rather than large groups of the same plant, throughout the year, then a cottage garden has been made. The challenge is to create a cohesive garden which gives constant interest and delight, ensuring that such random planting does not end up a formless mess.

An important initial consideration is to define and identify good cottage plants by looking at them in the context of how they are to be arranged within the confines of the garden. Cottages are essentially rural dwellings and, as such, their gardens will reflect the countryside where flower colours, shapes and sizes are seemingly random. Colour is an essential ingredient here, particularly since flowers play such a key role but, where colours are jumbled, there will be clashes and disharmony unless each fragment of colour is small enough to be lost in the general scheme. The best cottage plants, therefore, provide plenty of colour, but present it in small dots. Thus, a field poppy which

GREAT HERBACEOUS PLANTS FOR COTTAGE GARDENS

Winter: snowdrops (*Galanthus nivalis*); Christmas roses (*Helleborus niger*); winter aconites (*Aconitum*); *Crocus chrysanthus*.

ORIENTAL POPPIES WITH *ALLIUM AFLATUNENSE* AND *VERBASCUM PHOENICEUM*.

Above: A rustic arch furnished with climbing roses makes a welcoming approach to a front door. Lavender lines the path, providing summer fragrance; the hedge outline is softened by cranesbills flopping over it.

Opposite: This cottage garden is planted to look like a flowery meadow. The myriad small flowers create a mottled effect, soft in general view but with surprisingly strong colours working effectively together because the colour saturation is so low overall.

produces fifty small blooms in a season is preferable to an identically coloured *Papaver bracteatum*, which produces a dozen blooms that are three times the size.

In most cottages, the emphasis tends to be on herbaceous plants, often with a good proportion of annuals. This is not to say that outline is unimportant and we will study the choice of good outline plants shortly – but contrived hedges, small enclosures to create separate rooms and other self-conscious structures are not part of the cottage picture. What is the picture? As we have seen, it could be a simple pattern of paths or even a single path, bordered by a flowery expanse, with perhaps a few vegetables and fruit trees on the periphery of the garden. This sounds pretty enough, but the aim is to ensure that the 'flowery expanse' stays flowery for most of the year, without looking a mess in autumn, boring in winter or so bright in summer that you cannot bear to look at it without sunglasses. All in all, quite a tall order!

Spring: coloured primroses such as *Primula* 'Wanda' and border auriculas; botanical species of tulips, arabis, doronicums; honesty (*Lunaria rediviva*); sweet violets (*Viola odorata*); columbines (*Aquilegia*); Shirley poppies (*Papaver rhoeas*).

Summer: larkspurs (*Consolida ambigua*), cornflowers (*Centaurea cyanus*), calendulas, turkscap lilies (*Lilium martagon*), dwarf sunflowers (*Helianthus* 'Capenoch Star'), small-flowered dahlias; *Leucanthemum* 'Wirral Supreme'; mallows (*Lavatera*); alpine and old-fashioned border pinks (*Dianthus*).

Autumn: crocosmias; schizostylis; *Aster divaricatus*.

Year-round: violas and small pansies; herbs such as sage, parsley, thyme, rosemary, oregano, tarragon, borage and lovage; modern border pinks.

COTTAGE TREES AND SHRUBS

Having defined the cottage garden, for the purposes of this book, as being composed largely of herbaceous planting, it is now important to return to our original theme that planting is made up of the three main constituents – outline, understorey and highlights. These principles apply as much to cottage gardens as to any other, even if the outline consists of but one tree or shrub, and even if the highlight plants are sometimes in danger of being lost in the glorious muddle.

My model cottage garden would have at least a portion of its jumbled borders shaded by an old, gnarled apple tree. Its trunk, leaning gracefully towards the sun, would be covered in lichens and in its winter branches there would be a generous bunch of mistletoe to provide the necessary Christmas sprig for kissing under. Varieties of fruit are considered in more detail in the next chapter (see page 61), but, if using a lone tree, there is little to beat the apple, with its understated but beautiful spring blossom, pink in bud, opening white, its bountiful autumn crop and its gnarled winter outline, standing guard, like an old friend, against the weather.

Ornamental apples and fruiting crabs are almost as good as cropping apples, and, in time, can develop into shapely trees. The object, especially in a new garden, is to achieve maturity as quickly as possible and for that you need a tree or trees which are reasonably shapely even when quite young. My favourite fruiting crab, combining beauty with utility, is *Malus* 'John Downie', not only for its pink-flushed white blossom, but also for the scarlet and yellow autumn fruits which look so good on the tree you can hardly bring yourself to pick them. This is a relatively vigorous variety and, when I acquired a light standard specimen some time ago, in order to make it grow older-looking more quickly, I cut out the top as soon as I had planted it, leaving five lower branches. These I subsequently encouraged to grow long by pruning out the side-growth each summer. The result, after five years, is a fine, open tree which looks a good deal older than it really is.

Other deciduous cottage trees could include cherries such as *Prunus* 'Morello', which combines fruit with beauty and is largely self-pollinating, or any of the ornamental cherries or perhaps hawthorns (*Crataegus*), which grow into graceful shapes without needing extensive pruning. In a restricted space, the cherry 'Umineko', a small columnar tree, could be most effective: its autumn colour is good and the white spring blossom, consisting of mid-sized, single flowers – is exquisite.

An alternative or, perhaps, an additional outline plant for a cottage garden might be an evergreen tree. As in so many planting situations, holly (*Ilex*) is a good choice – indeed, few woody evergreen plants are quite so versatile. Holly can be left natural or pruned to any shape, or it can be trimmed to keep it small but natural-looking, or can even be crafted into a hedge. In some of the prettiest cottage gardens I remember seeing, the holly trees had been allowed to grow almost naturally in the front gardens, sometimes leaning their branches over old brick garden walls, the berries echoing the red of the brickwork. A pretty companion, perhaps even allowed to merge with the holly, is the snowy mespilus (*Amelanchier lamarckii*) whose leaves colour well and whose frail white spring blossom looks best against a dark evergreen background.

In a restricted garden area, there may not be room for a tree, in which case shrubs can be put to use as outline plants. The difference between a tree and a shrub is that the former usually has a single main trunk, or sometimes trunks, and is wider at the top than the base. A shrub is generally rounded in shape and tends to be wider at its base than on top. Certain shrub species lend themselves to being trained to become small trees: *Cotoneaster lacteus*, whose red

Left: The strawberry tree (*Arbutus unedo*), named for the resemblance of its fruits to the strawberry, can be pruned to a reasonable size to make a suitable tree for a small cottage garden.

Opposite: Traditional cottage gardens were productive, with plenty of fruit and vegetables to eke out a cottager's meagre wages. Here, an apple tree combines ornament with use, making a central feature for a bright planting of cottage flowers, including heartsease (*Viola tricolor*), poppies, cornflowers, foxgloves and such perennials as *Filpendula vulgaris*, snapdragons (*Antirrhinum*) and ragged robin (*Lychnis flos-cuculi*).

berries persist throughout winter, is a lax shrub which can be pruned to form a trunk and spreading branches. Just as elegant are forms of *C. x watereri*, whose berries are in the yellow, orange, amber or red range. One of the most vigorous forms is 'Rothschildianus', whose massed berries are a pale yellow. Portuguese laurel (*Prunus lusitanica*) is another example of a seemingly dull shrub which is surprisingly versatile. Eighteenth-century gardeners were familiar with its adaptability, using it for topiary specimens, such as large mushroom shapes, with thick trunks and convex tops. Such treatment might not be quite right for a cottage garden but the plant itself could be left to grow naturally, if there were space, or naturalistically pruned to a reduced size if dimensions were limited.

In mild or maritime areas, *Arbutus unedo* makes a ravishing cottage 'tree'. Though perfectly hardy at the roots, this species is vulnerable to sustained, heavy frost and can be cut to the ground in a very hard winter. But where the shrub is happy, the orange-red, sweet-tasting hairy fruits and creamy flowers appear together through the winter months. When mature, the trunk becomes wonderfully gnarled, its tan bark sloughing off to create a colourful winter effect.

53

THE COTTAGE-GARDEN BORDER

Having looked at outline plants, we should now complete the picture with some more specific ideas for the classic component of all cottage gardens – the border. Let us assume that we are lucky enough to have inherited the gnarled apple tree for our outline, and that this throws shade for part of the year over about a third of the area. In the spirit of the cottage garden, we will have trained not only a wild honeysuckle (*Lonicera periclymenum*) into it, but also the rambling rose 'Albertine', which we prevent from growing too large and which we intertwine with *Clematis* x *jackmanii* 'Superba'. That completes our outline planting, although we may dot sage, lavender, rosemary and perhaps a couple of moss roses about, almost at random, or in loose groups, to create a little permanent height. Some of the herbaceous plants we are using will in fact be big enough to create temporary outline during the growing season. The main objective is to develop as rich and varied an understorey as we can, bearing in mind the importance of year-round interest.

WINTER TO SPRING In the shady part of the border, *Helleborus foetidus* 'Wester Flisk' can be interplanted with snowdrops and the daffodil varieties 'February Gold', 'Jack Snipe' or 'Peeping Tom' with *Epimedium youngianum* 'Niveum' and perhaps *E. versicolor*. And in fuller light, we might grow *Omphalodes verna* or *O. cappadocica*, with a number of different primroses – all mixed up so they will hybridize – plus, nearer the back of the border, *Paeonia officinalis*, which will blend happily with blue columbines (*Aquilegia*) and late cottage tulips.

SUMMER Though we are not inhibited about colour, it makes sense to gather the plants into broadly related colour groupings, especially where certain simple associations are likely to work well. In early summer, and in dappled shade, for instance, the globeflower, *Trollius chinensis* 'Golden Queen' or 'Orange Princess', looks magnificent with the vivid golden-green of *Euphorbia palustris*, especially if there is *Iris sibirica* behind to introduce a sharp blue contrast. In fuller light, red and blue make a pleasing summer combination, perhaps selecting oriental poppies to go with blue lupins and delphiniums, especially the shorter, belladonna hybrids. Hot summer colours, using geums or potentillas, with such red dahlias as 'Bishop of Llandaff' dotted around to make burning highlights, can be enhanced with the cool, silvery foliage of *Anaphalis margaritacea* or silvery artemisias.

To heighten the midsummer crescendo, we could introduce tender perennials into the gaps: the blue daisy (*Felicia amelloides*), for example, looks pretty among border pinks or with pink argyranthemums. And hardy annuals, even if they push your colour mix beyond the limits of good taste, are a worthwhile investment. They are easy to grow, good-natured in their requirements and, if it all becomes too much for your sensibilities, can be taken out with minimal loss. Bright, happy marigolds (who could dislike their cheerful colours?); nasturtiums which scramble about,

Right: A blend of showy annuals, perennials and wildflowers – weeds, even – produces a rich midsummer climax in warm colours. The goldenrods, perennial asters and huge sunflowers will ensure a continuation of colour and in winter the teasels (currently blooming) will make a pleasing outline with their dead stems and seedheads.

Left: Hellebores and snowdrops are winter favourites, not only for cottage gardens but for every style of garden. With carefully made selections, it is possible in all but the most frost-prone regions to have them in bloom from early winter through to mid-spring.

SMALL PRODUCTIVE GARDENS

Nothing is quite as delicious as food you have produced yourself. A lettuce that has been picked young and plump, washed and eaten within the hour; potatoes so new and tender that their skins slough off as soon as you handle them, strawberries so fragrant that your mouth waters as you pick them – all these experiences are possible for anyone who has a few square metres of soil.

It would of course be unrealistic to suppose that a tiny garden will feed a family of six, but it is possible to produce a surprising amount of food from a very small plot, given reasonable soil, full light and a temperate climate. The level of production you achieve depends, naturally, on how much effort you are prepared to make, and on how much beauty you want to sacrifice. Most people with small gardens merely wish to raise a few salad greens, have a few fresh herbs available and, perhaps, harvest an item or two of fruit, provided it comes from a decorative tree that graces their garden.

But, if you want to go all out for heavy cropping, you will be astonished at how productive a small garden can be. Even with minimal space, it is possible to raise an excitingly varied selection of fresh vegetables, fruit and herbs through the greater part of the year. Even on a small terrace it is feasible, with the use of growing bags and other containers, to produce a significant supply of such vegetables as aubergines and tomatoes as well as salad greens, cucumbers and peppers. Small quantities of fruits can be raised in large pots – figs love growing in containers, for instance – and, if you have a warm, sunny wall, you could even try growing your own grapes.

Above: Traditional rhubarb forcing pots are back in fashion today, following the revival of earlier kitchen-garden styles. They make an ornamental feature in vegetable gardens, before being taken off to reveal the soft pink stems and bright green leaves of the emerging young rhubarb.

Opposite: Even the smallest garden can produce considerable quantities of fresh produce without looking untidy. Vegetables and salads are interplanted with such herbs as marjoram and parsley here, giving an effect reminiscent of a small knot garden. The standard bay trees contribute to the garden's formality.

MAXIMIZING THE OUTPUT

At the core of successful food production are four key factors: the right timing, maximizing fertility, careful planning and good husbandry.

TIMING It is often said that the difference between a good farmer and a bad one is a fortnight. What this means is that the good husbandman will sow seed, take cuttings, transplant and harvest fruit at precisely the right moment. It may well be just as disastrous being premature, with such sensitive activities as seed sowing, as being tardy: too early, and you are sowing into cold soil, probably into an ill-prepared seed bed, and will experience poor germination; too late and your yields will be lower than they might have been since the crop has not had optimum time to mature.

Having a greenhouse will help you to extend your activities and to have far more fun with your horticulture. The growing season starts a great deal earlier under glass and raising seedlings ready for spring planting is one of the most satisfying winter jobs. But here, planning will be even more crucial: from a few seeds, sprinkled on to compost, will come young plants which will need to be protected for weeks, perhaps even months, during which time they will be growing and therefore demanding increasing amounts of space.

Preparing the ground outdoors well ahead of time is a way of easing pressure in the greenhouse. Cloches, sheets of plastic or even horticultural fleece can all be used as part of the soil warming process. Cloches keep the ground dry and also warm it so that seeds sown directly outdoors, protected by them, will germinate more quickly. And a cold frame is a boon too, if you have lots of seedlings or young plants, not only to provide extra protection for them during their most vulnerable stages, but also to run through the gradual process of hardening them off – that is, acclimatizing them for life outdoors.

FERTILITY Feeding the soil and keeping it in good heart is essential for top cropping. Soil is very like a living organism in itself: in composition it consists of mineral and organic particles containing billions of micro-organisms and, most important, a mix of water and air. Water coats each individual particle of soil but air must fill the spaces between them. To provide all the essentials for plant growth, the soil needs to be structurally sound – that is, loose and friable enough to allow roots to penetrate easily; to carry oxygen for the tiny single-cell root hairs to survive; and it needs to have each discrete particle coated in a film of water in which mineral nutrient salts are dissolved. A flower garden also needs its soil to be in good heart, but this demands less fertility than in the case of food production, where successive harvests remove from the soil its sustenance, mainly in the form of mineral nutrients, which must be replaced somehow.

From a practical point of view, this means that you must add composted organic material (or rotted farmyard manure if you are lucky enough to obtain

Below: Beehives make a decorative addition to the kitchen or flower garden, and if you become a real bee-keeper, your fruit will benefit from the bees' pollinating activities, your flowers will produce more seed and you could use the natural honey to sweeten your stewed rhubarb.

any) to your soil each season. You will also need to replenish the nutrient levels by adding sources of all the main fertilizing agents – namely, nitrogen, phosphorus and potassium – and perhaps, from time to time, such lesser minerals as magnesium and iron too.

A good way of ensuring rich, fertile soil, especially if the naturally occurring material is not very bountiful, is to develop raised beds. By constructing a system of wooden frames with sides up to about 30cm (12in) high, you can build up the ground level within them by incorporating organic material from such sources as rotted garden compost, leafmould, well-rotted manure, composted lawn mowings – or a mix of all these. It will take several seasons to complete the build-up of fertility, but your efforts to intensify production will be rewarded with a steady increase, not only in yields, but also in the quality of your produce.

PLANNING For maximum production, good planning is essential. If the ground is empty for any reason other than that a crop has just been harvested from it, this represents a loss of potential. Double cropping helps to produce more yield per square metre (yard): a winter crop of cabbage, for example, could be followed immediately after its harvest in early spring by a new planting of lettuces, which will mature within about three months. These are removed, making room for a summer planting of leeks which will be ready for harvest towards the end of the following winter. That kind of planning ensures that every centimetre or inch of space is utilized efficiently.

Close planting can raise yields too, especially if you are able to eat the thinnings! Carrots, for example, can be thinned – though this increases the risk of carrot fly attack – giving you baby carrots to eat before the main crop matures. Root crops like swedes or turnips are edible as greens, when very young and picked as thinnings.

Inter-planting developing crops with catch crops is a help too. Radish, lettuce and other salad crops,

inter-sown between rows of such longer-term crops as cabbage, Brussels sprouts or celery, provide extra food. Conversely, young tomato plants, aubergines or peppers could be slipped in between maturing leafy vegetables, such as spinach, which will be harvested before they are able adversely to affect the new plants.

HUSBANDRY One aspect of so-called organic gardening is that, without chemical aids, the success of the garden depends more heavily on good management. In practice, this means that you need to keep a watchful eye on your plants so that you will be able to anticipate potential problems and circumvent them. Dry weather, for example, calls for water, but a wise grower will have mulched the soil to conserve moisture long before the effects of drought put the plants under stress. A good gardener also knows what diseases and pests are likely and takes precautionary measures to deter them.

Above: Catch crops of carrots and Lollo Rossa lettuce are here interplanted between rows of longer-term vegetables such as cabbages and beans. Orange Californian poppies look gorgeous scattered among the purple foliage of red cabbage and beet.

Right: Nasturtiums are both decorative and edible. They can be plucked when young and tossed into green salads to bring them to life with their colour and peppery flavour. Their vivid blooms and rounded leaves make a pretty contrast with the bluish foliage of young cabbages.

Opposite: Especially in small plots, productive gardens must combine ornament with use. Outline in this decorative kitchen garden is provided by fruit trees trained into an arch; extra colour comes from the flower border flanking the vegetable bed.

COMBINING PRODUCE WITH ORNAMENTALS

The great majority of owners of small gardens, if they produce food at all, do it very much as a sideline. Most people, for example, will have a selection of herbs somewhere in their garden and a good many like to set aside a small area for growing greens, but one of the most effective means of having a little fresh produce available, at least in summer, is to combine food production with ornamental gardening.

With a cottage garden, vegetable and fruit production go together naturally – indeed, flowers could easily play second fiddle to crops without spoiling the landscape. We have already seen that the outline plants in a cottage garden could be apple trees, but a small bed of top fruit, if there is enough space, could also form the spinal part of any garden's overall design. The natural tendency is to grow plants in rows, but there is no unbreakable law that says this has to be the way. Arranged artistically as part of a mixed border, carrots, brassicas, broad beans and

squashes or courgettes all contribute much beauty while they mature. Broad, waxy blue-green cabbage leaves, for example, associate as beautifully with the ferny foliage of carrots as they do with the similar leaves of love-in-a-mist (*Nigella*). The big yellow blooms of courgettes and squashes are beautiful, and though the large leaves may frequently hide them, at least they are shapely and handsomely marked.

It is important, however, to be practical. If a vegetable crop becomes a focal point in the cottage border, you will need to have an impressive replacement to fill the yawning gap that appears when you harvest it. Unlike the majority of ornamental plants, vegetable crops need special treatment as they develop: root crops have to be thinned, potatoes and celery need to be earthed up and runner beans to be trained up supports. It is essential that all these plants are not merely accessible, but that they can receive the attention they need without spoiling the rest of the garden.

In a more formal design, food production is in some respects simpler. Indeed, the first formal gardens were probably nothing more than ordered ways of producing crops. In medieval times, the food and physic gardens of the monasteries were, in essence, simplified versions of the grand parterres that evolved after the Renaissance. Most had a cruciform layout, with systems of raised beds and a mix of medicinal plants, vegetables and flowers were raised. The modern equivalent (though more popular in gardening books and at horticultural shows than in reality, I suspect) is the miniature *potager*. This is a small formal area, made decorative in line and form, using food plants rather than ornamentals. The effect is very appealing, especially at flower shows where everything is brought to perfection together, but it does need, in real life, masterly planning and control. If you have a greenhouse and cold frames, with plenty of young plants coming on, you can replace crops constantly as you harvest. The amount you are able to produce will astound you.

FRUIT FOR A SMALL GARDEN

The tendency, in a small space, is to go for soft fruit, such as raspberries and currants, because the plants are relatively small, in relation to trees which take up too much space. But soft fruit is not especially decorative and does in fact occupy quite a lot of ground for a comparatively low yield. But then, it is hard to beat the flavour of absolutely fresh raspberries, picked and eaten within minutes. And can you ever buy such freshness? The decision is whether to sacrifice space for a crop that is not exactly ravishing to look at. While you ponder the dilemma, remember that rows of raspberry canes need to be about 1.5metres (5ft)

Below: Gooseberries grown as standards permit more space beneath their branches for low-growing salad crops or vegetables. Beauty is provided for here as well, by including bulbs of *Allium christophii*, with their tall, starry heads.

apart. Gooseberries and currants can be forced to save space by growing them as cordons – that is, trained on wires – 1.5metres (5ft) apart and set at 45° angles.

The prettiest soft fruit of all is the strawberry, which can be grown as a container plant or in a bed. The white flowers, with their yellow centres, and the three-lobed leaves are beautiful and, when the fruits are ripening, pale at first, then flushing to a deep red, they look so good that it seems a crime to pick them. This double contribution makes strawberries truly great plants for small gardens. And if you select late- and repeat-cropping varieties, and make use of cloches for early harvest, you will lengthen the season by providing fruits in spring, summer and autumn.

Top fruit trees are beautiful too, as we have seen in the chapter on cottage gardens (see page 49). Using varieties on dwarfing rootstocks enables you to fit more into a confined space, as small free-standing trees, as cordons or even as tiny, step-over (I call them trip-over) apples, trained as very low espalier trees at around 45cm (18in) in height. Full-sized espalier apples and pears are a much more practical way of providing a decorative and productive boundary to your kitchen garden, or indeed to the garden as a whole. Pruning them may look complicated but it could hardly be simpler: all you do is cut the newly developed shoots back to the main stems, in midsummer, leaving stumps with about three buds on each. These will develop into next year's fruiting spurs.

Finally, do not overlook the benefits of a warm wall. In winter, a wall which faces the sun for much of the day will store residual heat overnight, sometimes keeping the plants that are trained on it free of frost, even when ground temperatures approach freezing. Peaches, nectarines, apricots and dessert plums are all good wall fruits in a cold area, as are pears and figs. It is possible to train young trees into a fan shape, but it is much easier to buy them ready-trained, so that all you need do is prune back to the original branches in subsequent years.

THE BEST VEGETABLES AND SALADS

Since almost any vegetable is worth growing if you enjoy eating it, here it may be more helpful to suggest those best omitted from the small kitchen garden, rather than listing varieties, many of which are in any case constantly being outmoded by improved ones.

Assuming space is limited, always select dwarf or low-growing varieties of: broad beans, peas, mange-tout peas, snap beans, cabbages and so on. Where space is severely restricted, grow only those crops that taste so much better fresh than purchased: sweetcorn, for example, though a space hogger, is so much more delectable if boiled within moments of being harvested. Most mature root crops are as good purchased as home-grown, but not in their baby state, since young carrots, turnips or beets have such a short shelf life. Maincrop potatoes taste much the same, whether field-grown or raised at home, but baby new potatoes change their characteristics within hours of harvest and are therefore good to raise at home. Since they occupy the ground for only a few weeks, they can be followed with a later summer crop. Maincrop potatoes take six months to mature.

Leafy vegetables and salads always taste better if home grown. Salads can be sown in succession and, nowadays, most seedsmen offer mixes of seed so that different varieties can be sown at the same time. Take advantage of this and have a selection of 'cut and come again' plants which will go on yielding food over long periods. Ruby chard, a leaf vegetable decorative enough for the border, seems to go on producing the generous oar-shaped leaves which are so delicious when young in summer. In winter, purple-sprouting broccoli or even cattle kale keep on regenerating new shoots as often as the mature ones are cut, making

them superb winter vegetables, rich in nutrients and decidedly tasty when lightly steamed.

Perennial vegetables are less easy to justify from the point of view of space utilization. Globe artichokes, for example, take up a great deal of space for the amount of food they yield, but they are handsome and decorative plants as well as being delicious to eat: you have to make a choice. Asparagus, too, is unsurpassable when absolutely fresh but uses a lot of ground, which can be difficult to keep weed-free. Furthermore, you cannot utilize the space occupied by asparagus for any other plant, throughout the year, so that short but delectable harvest comes at quite a price.

Above: A tiny corner of a garden is turned into a productive space by planting cabbages and Brussels sprouts, with lettuces bordering the path. Even the wall behind is furnished with runner beans. Though hardly a market garden, it looks orderly and provides freshly picked vegetables and salads now and again.

SMALL WATER GARDENS

In any garden setting, water brings an extra dimension. With its reflective qualities, it creates a subsidiary light source at ground level, illuminating plants and objects near its surface, and it enhances the beauty of waterside plants and buildings because they are mirrored in its surface. Water also increases the apparent dimensions of a garden by making a huge void in which the heavens are reflected.

In the fabled Moorish gardens of the Alhambra, in Granada, Spain, water was used, as far back as the twelfth century, to reflect the facades of buildings. Rills are fed with springs engineered to pour into a long, rectangular pool, creating exactly the right degree of rippling on the surface of the water. If you stand in a certain position, looking along the gently moving water, you cannot tell which columns are reflected and which are real, because the place where reflection meets reality is smudged by the ripples. The effect is of a castle suspended in the air – about as near to heaven as the Moorish architects could get!

A water feature can totally transform a small garden. Even in the most restricted of spaces, a small fountain or bubbling spring brings the landscape to life with its tinkling and moving. Water is also wildlife-friendly, not only as a habitat for aquatic animals, but for other species to come to drink and bathe: in early spring, before there is much nectar about, you will see honey bees drinking from a pond and birds make frequent visits, either to drink or to dunk themselves into the water. The animals of the night drink at the pond too, whether they be hedgehogs or other small mammals.

Above: This intriguing water feature brings wit as well as soothing sounds to a small garden. Shells depict the head of Mercury, the ancient Greeks' winged messenger, and from his mouth water trickles down a series of dished metal saucers into a contained pool below.

Opposite: Thick, lush planting almost conceals this water feature but the coolness of the colours – mostly green or variegated foliage – and the presence of ferns and grasses go perfectly with a watery theme.

THE VIRTUES OF GREAT WATER PLANTS

A pond or stream on its own is a sterile object and is only made beautiful by the plants that populate the water, the water margins and the area in which the pond is set. Many water plants can grow huge and untidy, which is fine on a lake site but disastrous in a confined garden. Great water plants for small gardens must be better behaved than that, or must be so ravishingly beautiful that they are forgiven for an untidy aftermath. Small size is not necessarily what we are after, however. Many large, bold species make wonderful small-garden subjects, their stature towering over everything else in a dramatic way. The rhubarb relative, *Rheum palmatum* 'Rubrum', for example, has huge, puckered leaves which, as they expand, throw considerable shade. The flower spikes, when they arrive, are even more dramatic, zooming up in a few days to a height of two metres (6½ft), then erupting into an explosion of tiny pink or creamy flowers.

Below: The statue in this small water feature provides a permanent focal point but in summer, the effect is amplified by the bold blooms of the African arum lily (*Zantedeschia aethiopica*). Though this plant is tender, if it is submerged, the roots should be safe from frost.

Good water garden plants will die away gracefully, or will not object to being cut back early. They will stand well, not produce too much floppy foliage, and they will be decorative for a significant period. In the water itself, we must also look for interesting and attractive foliage, preferably with variation and contrasts in colour, texture and shape. In winter, when most water features look bleak, we want to be able to tidy the site and, perhaps, to remove most of the top growth. But for interest, it is important to have a dwarf willow or some other moisture-loving shrub or tree to provide a shapely contour or, at least, to give some relief from the flatness of the scene.

Certain plants are universally beneficial in any pond because they are important for helping to maintain the right ecological balance.

PLANTS WITH FLOATING LEAVES Plants whose foliage rests on the water surface are particularly important, especially in full sun, because they throw shade. Not only does this prevent the water from overheating, it also reduces the rate at which undesirable algae multiply. Thus, water lilies (*Nymphaea*) are not only pretty, but are almost essential for helping to keep the water clear. The water hawthorn (*Aponogeton distachyos*), a Southern African plant, also has floating leaves and pretty white, sweetly fragrant flowers.

OXYGENATING PLANTS Beneath the surface of the water, a healthy pond will be teeming with life. If you were to take a drop of water, put it on a slide and examine it under a microscope, you would see whole congregations of simple plants and animals. To thrive, these will need oxygen dissolved in the water. Fish, if they are present, will also consume dissolved oxygen, and will excrete nitrogenous waste which could pollute unless there are water plants to make use of it for their own growing requirements. Thus, it is important to have a thriving population of submerged green plants. Oxygenating weeds such as water crowfoot,

hornwort (*Ceratophyllum demersum*), starwort (*Callitriche verna*) and Canadian pondweed (*Elodea canadensis*) can all be used for this and to provide the right habitat for the other pond creatures. Even duckweed, the tiny plants that float to make a green scum on the surface, is beneficial in moderate quantities. For summer use in ponds where the fish population is a little higher than is strictly healthy, the water hyacinth (*Eichhornia crassipes*) is a marvellous absorber of nitrogenous waste. It is said to absorb other toxins too, the idea being that as the floating colonies expand, you keep removing plants and discarding them, diluting the toxins as you do so.

MARGINAL PLANTING Besides constituting the bulk of the water garden display, marginal plants provide important cover for creatures wishing to enter or leave the water. If, for example, you have frogs breeding in your pond, the adults will need rushes in which to hide. Smaller grasses such as *Hakonechloa macra* 'Aureola' and *Molinia caerulea* 'Variegata' are effective too. For the emerging froglets, at their most vulnerable as they take their first steps into the wide world, cover at the pondside will greatly increase their chances of survival. To set off reeds and grasses, try variegated ground ivy (*Glechoma hederacea*) or the pretty dead-nettles (*Lamium maculatum*).

Above: Thoughtful planting will soften the hard lines of a formal pond, especially one that is above ground, without losing the essential geometry of the design. Here, the sword-like leaves of irises contrast with the featheriness of fern foliage and that of *Acer palmatum*.

73

SMALL FORMAL POOLS

A formal pool is symmetrical in almost every case. Rectangles, sometimes with rounded ends, are the most popular shapes, but small formal water features could also include semi-circles, perhaps under a wall with a spigot of some kind trickling water into the pool. Rounded pools, with or without moving water, can make a central feature in a formal garden. Whatever its shape, if it is large enough, with a depth over part of it of at least 45cm (18in), it will be able to accommodate fish and all the other species associated with pond life. But there is in fact no need for a water feature to support life. A tiny fountain, with virtually no pool at all – nothing more than a bubbling spring that wells up over cobbles, or perhaps over the small

replica of a granite millstone – would be excellent where space is severely restricted or if there are small children at risk. Even a submerged sink, or a tub on the terrace, can be made into a tiny water feature which, even though it may not be a precious wildlife resource, will still provide a taste of the special magic that water brings to a garden.

Planting in a formal pool presents rather more of a challenge than with informal ponds. For a start, it is impossible to arrange the plants themselves formally – they will always grow naturally, softening hard lines, rather than appearing in neat rows or blocks. Every plant you introduce will blur the line and obscure the geometry of your pool, so if you wish to keep the lines of your design fairly severe, you must limit your choice. And yet, with careful placing, a plant specimen, growing naturally, can emphasize the formal lines of the rest of the pool.

Below: The bold, shapely foliage of *Rodgersia* makes a pleasing contrast with the decking in this water garden where differing levels create interest. In turn, the large foliage associates with reed-like irises to give a natural waterside effect.

MARGINAL PLANTS

Plants with an upright stance and vertical leaves are wonderful contributors to the effect of a formal pool. Irises, particularly those with variegated foliage, make a fully vertical statement, accentuated, in variegated species, by the stripes of their leaves. You will need only one plant in a small pool, and this should be confined to a basket so that it does not spread. *Iris laevigata* is one of the finest, with big, blue, white or bicoloured flowers in early summer. It comes with plain green or variegated leaves. An alternative is the variegated form of yellow flag (*Iris pseudacorus* 'Variegata'), a fine foliage plant with bold green and golden-cream stripes. The flowers are daffodil yellow and the heavy seedheads add later interest. Other marginals with prettily coloured foliage include Bowles golden sedge (*Carex stricta* 'Aurea'), which can be planted with the purple-leaved *Lobelia cardinalis* whose tall spires of dazzling scarlet flowers are set off so well by the brooding bronze to purple foliage.

To offset the plants with narrow leaves and an erect habit, there are marginals whose foliage is generously broad. The white arum (*Zantedeschia aethiopica*) has beautiful dark green, broad foliage and the flowers make exquisite bonus specimens through summer. A pretty alternative – or a companion to the arums – is the pickerel weed (*Pontederia cordata*), which also has pleasing broad leaves and, in late summer, intense blue flowers. But the great thing, with formal pools, is not to overdo it. Keeping the planting minimal will not only help to maintain the formal feel but will ensure that the few plants used are appreciated more fully.

IN THE WATER

The object must be to retain as much reflective surface as possible by keeping it clear of foliage but, at the same time, providing enough shading in summer to maintain a well-balanced and healthy pond. Small water lilies are ideal and, of these, *Nymphaea pygmaea* is best for very shallow water. A pretty alternative to

water lilies is an unrelated water plant known as the buckbean (*Nymphoides peltata*). This is frighteningly vigorous, soon forming wide expanses of floating leaves among which the prettily fringed yellow flowers appear for most of summer. But, as long as it is confined to a small pond, it is a simple matter to keep pulling out the surplus and composting it.

Submerged plants that rear up out of the water can make handsome statements in a small pond and one of my favourites is a British wild plant, the arrowhead (*Sagittaria sagittifolia*), whose white flowers are produced in sprays in midsummer. The solid appearance of its arrow-shaped foliage could be offset by the vivid emerald, feathery leaves of the parrot feather (*Miriophyllum proserpinacoides*). This plant is a lazy gardener's dream – you simply throw pieces into the water and they float, grow and expand; the unwanted surplus makes good compost. As with the marginal plants, the secret, with a formal pool, is to keep the planting as simple and as severe as you can – but to enjoy the plants you select!

Left: Even the tiniest of gardens or courtyards provide opportunities for a water feature. Here, a modest, water-filled container creates a small focal point in a shady corner. The variegated foliage of the euonymus surrounding the container helps to brighten the gloom and provide colour and interest in winter.

INFORMAL SMALL PONDS

An informal pond can take whatever shape you like, as long as it imitates nature. Streamlets, rills, shallow plashes, pebble beaches and muddy zones can all be incorporated, provided the whole fits comfortably into the allotted area. If you can manage to include a shallow sloping side or a tiny intermediate area for some wetland plants, the effect will be much better than a kidney-shaped pondlet sunk into a lawn or terrace.

MARGINAL PLANTS

By using individual planting baskets – and these are easily the best means of growing water plants – you can go for a glorious selection of marginals, many of which will also grow in the wet ground at the edge of a sloping side. Such 'amphibious' species include wildflowers like kingcup (*Caltha palustris*), purple loosestrife (*Lythrum salicaria*), *Iris sanguinea* and the gorgeous Japanese iris (*I. kaempferi*) with its huge, flattened blooms in soft blues and lavenders. Among these taller plants, you can arrange for such trailers and creepers as the Cambridge-blue water forget-me-not (*Myosotis scorpioides*), creeping Jenny (*Lysimachia nummularia*) and the brighter coloured monkey flowers (*Mimulus*), many of which are charming, particularly *M. cupreus*, *M. lewisii*, 'Whitecroft Scarlet' and the gorgeous pink and cream 'Andean Nymph'.

IN THE WATER

You can afford to splurge on the water plants, bearing in mind that in high summer you may have to do some thinning. The choice of water lilies will depend on the pond size: *Nymphaea* 'James Brydon', with double pink flowers, is vigorous and dependable; 'Chromatella' is a fancy pale yellow and 'Masaniello' pink and cream.

I have a soft spot for European wild flowers such as water crowfoot (*Ranunculus aquatilis*), an excellent oxygenator with pretty white buttercup flowers held up on little stems above the water in spring. More gorgeous, but needing acid water, is the water violet (*Hottonia palustris*) whose lilac blooms also rise from the water like magic and appear suspended above the shimmering surface. A batch of oxygenating weed helps to balance the pond and provides a home for dragonfly larvae, small fish, water snails and the myriad smaller organisms needed for a balanced pond. One which is attractive below the surface, where its leaves are often silvered with oxygen bubbles, is the shining pondweed (*Potamogeton crispus*). Canadian pondweed (*Elodea canadensis*), hornwort (*Ceratophyllum demersum*), and starwort (*Callitriche verna*) also make pretty submerged colonies. And, for extra shading, try floating plants such as fairy moss (*Azolla filiculoides*) or even the tender water hyacinth (*Eichhornia crassipes*).

PLANTS AROUND THE POND

One of the problems associated with small ponds is making the surrounding planting scheme blend comfortably with the water feature. The ground around a wild, natural pond is usually damp, with marshy areas, whereas in most small gardens the pond has been artificially added, so the surrounding land is too dry to look authentically boggy. But there is a collection of plants which are happy in ordinary soil but have the appearance of bog plants, making it possible to create a bogside feel, using plants tolerant of dry conditions.

Hostas and ferns look as though they need moisture but they are perfectly content in ordinary soil. The big, bold hostas such as *H. sieboldiana* 'Blue Angel' or the green-leaved 'Honeybells' look lovely set off with such ferns as *Polystichum setiferum*, especially the evergreen garden form 'Divisilobum', with feathery foliage. Bergenia has a lush appearance, especially *B. crassifolia*; in semi-shade, the form 'Bressingham White' has flowers that stand out well, but for vividness of hue you need *B.* 'Abendglut', whose flowers are a startling purplish-cerise.

Right: An informal pond at the height of summer. Plants may grow so vigorously along the margins that the water itself can almost disappear. This enhances, rather than detracts from, the natural appearance and, from a practical point of view, improves the aquatic environment by making it more wildlife-friendly. As well as wild species, the water is surrounded by cranesbills, delphiniums and other garden favourites.

A FORMAL COURTYARD POOL

In a small garden, a formal pool becomes the focal point of the design. The rectangular shape is echoed by the straight edges to the surrounding borders and walls, creating a symmetry which, without plants to blur hard edges and soften the focus, could feel contrived and uncomfortable. The paved area is spacious enough to relax and enjoy the peaceful ambience but there is still ample room for a collection of plants on the walls, in the main border and in the water. Containers add extra planting opportunities and allow for instant changes to be made; they also become decorative features in their own right.

The pond is relatively large in relation to the space available, giving it a special prominence and allowing the reflective properties of the water to increase the sense of light and space. Planting here is severe – almost minimal – with but two marginal plants (the irises), a couple of water lilies and some oxygenating plants below the surface. In contrast, the border to one side is furnished with plants selected for their bold, luxuriant foliage, including bamboo, the ornamental rhubarb and skunk cabbage (*Lysichiton*), helping to create an almost tropical feel. The shapely hosta foliage in the border at the foot of the wall echoes the leafy appearance of the courtyard, while the choice of *Zantedeschia* for the container heightens the somewhat exotic effect.

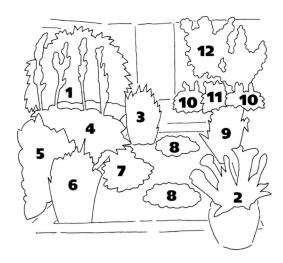

THE PLANTS

1	*Fargesia nitida*	**7**	*Aponogeton distachyos*
2	*Zantedeschia aethiopica*	**8**	*Nymphaea* 'Hermine'
3	*Iris laevigata*		and 'Baroness Orczy'
4	*Rheum palmatum*	**9**	*Iris pseudacorus*
	'Atrosanguineum'	**10**	*Hosta fortunei*
5	*Lysichiton americanus*	**11**	*Hosta crispula*
6	*Iris pseudacorus*	**12**	*Clematis* 'Niobe'
	'Variegata'		

SMALL VERTICAL GARDENS

In a small space, the vertical garden frequently occupies as great, or an even greater area than the horizontal. If you imagine a rectangular plot, 15m (50ft) long by 6m (20ft) wide, at the back of a terraced town house, it may well have three boundary walls or fences 2m (6½ft) high, with the back wall of the house rising to, perhaps, 8m (26ft). The total area of vertical planting opportunity this creates runs to 90 square metres – which is precisely the ground dimensions of the garden, give or take a few square metres for doorways and windows. If you add to that the opportunity offered by arches, a pergola, pillars, posts or perhaps trees which could accommodate climbing plants, it is easy to see what an important role vertical planting plays in a small garden.

In addition to supplying new planting opportunities, gardening on a vertical plane also provides a varied range of growing conditions. Walls which face the sun hold residual heat, raising temperatures slightly at night and elevating them markedly by day. Thus they create a microclimate which increases the chances of survival of marginally hardy species and which hastens the ripening, not only of fruit, but also of the buds of such superb climbers as wisteria, *Campsis radicans* and *Schizophragma integrifolium*, so that they flower all the more profusely. Walls that face away from the sun reduce the extremes, both of high and low temperatures, and reduce light levels so that species which, in nature, inhabit quiet woodland or shaded hillsides will thrive, whereas they might burn up in the open. East-facing walls, enjoying clear sunlight in the morning, are fine for spring plants which enjoy full light, but which must not be drawn on too fast. West-facing walls, often the most desirable of all, enjoy the most bountiful of climates, with warm afternoon sunshine but no extremes of temperature.

Above: Harmonious colours but contrasting flower shapes make a charming partnership, as *Clematis* 'Dawn' intertwines with the honeysuckle *Lonicera periclymenum* 'Belgica'.

Opposite: The beauty of mellow stonework can be enhanced by the thoughtful use of climbers and wall plants. Here climbing roses, honeysuckle and Virginia creeper (*Parthenocissus quinquefolia*) surround mullioned windows, their colours making a good contrast with the campanula planted in the ground below.

VERTICAL GARDENING

Furnishing the walls, fences and other plant-supporting devices transforms the design of a small garden as well as introducing into it a wider range of growing conditions. Plants are brought up to eye level, so that flowers can be enjoyed without having to stoop, their fragrances are fed through open windows and softening shade is brought to part of the garden. Screens can be developed from plants, creating a tapestry which, besides blocking off a view to create privacy, can become a delightful planting feature in itself, changing through the year, but always green and living.

The principles of planting the vertical plane differ from those laid down at the beginning of this book (see page 14) only in that we can assume the outline to be there already – the 'outline', in this case, will be

Below: Careful planting is as important on the vertical plane as on the horizontal. Here, the purple-leaved vine (*Vitis vinifera* 'Purpurea') associates perfectly with the royal blue flowers of *Clematis* x *jackmanii* 'Superba'.

what the plants actually grow on! The understorey, when it is created, will be on its side: it will consist of a pleasant background or infill, which runs through a series of gentle seasonal changes and which manages alterations in mood and texture from one area to another. Highlight plants will play an even stronger role than they do on the ground. Those climbing species that dazzle with their displays will tend to dominate the entire garden for short periods. Wisteria grown against the south side of a house, for example, commands attention for the whole of its flowering period. But if you can blend that gorgeous purple-blue with the acid yellow of *Fremontodendron* 'California Glory', or the softer primrose-yellow of the Banksian rose (*R. banksiae* 'Lutea'), the display will be longer and more memorable.

Effective though vertical gardening can be, its disadvantage is that the plants have to find a way of coping with gravity. Apart from a small selection of species which are happy to scramble upwards with their own self-clinging devices, the majority will only give optimum displays if a little trouble is taken with their support. On walls and fences, the easiest way to achieve this is to install wires, trellis or netting. The simplest system to construct is a series of horizontal wires pegged to the wall at 2m (6½ft) intervals, strongly tensioned and held at least 2.5cm (1in) away from the wall by vine eyes – long screws or nails with eyes at their ends. Tie the leading shoots loosely into these wires as the plants develop; once established, climbers will usually cling to the support wires unaided.

Climbing shrubs, particularly roses, benefit from being pruned into a fan shape, then tied into their supports each year. Take out old growths, but tie back any long stems that have developed the previous season, since these are most likely to flower profusely. Try not to cross any stems over and spread out the 'fan' as evenly as possible. If late-flowering clematis are grown among the roses, they can be pruned back hard when the roses are rearranged, to encourage new leads: these

will bear flowers from the second half of the summer. Winter is a good time to take stock of densely tangled climbers and hard-prune them into shape. A severe pruning will often invigorate rugged varieties and enable you to enforce a little more discipline.

THE ROLE OF WALL PLANTS

Wall plants are those plants, mostly shrubs, which form the bulk of the vertical planting. Though not necessarily climbing, they lend themselves to wall culture, where they can be used to create a framework on which to base the rest of the planting; they might just as easily be furnishing a fence, softening the lines of a pergola or covering an outbuilding. They have enough strength, with support, to carry a range of subsidiary plants (the climbers) and are selected not only as good companions for the climbers, but also to work well with one another. It is possible for a group of wall plants to merge into a kind of vegetative tapestry which relies on a series of bursts of interest throughout the year.

Above: Abundant vertical planting has turned this small seating area into an attractive bower. The wealth of foliage makes for a cooling, shady effect with roses for fragrance and for colour. *Clematis viticella* 'Etoile Violette' will be in bloom from around the longest day until the first frosts. Container-grown plants complete the picture.

SUPERLATIVE WALL PLANTS

The most effective way of planting the vertical plane is to build up a composition in which the framework consists of wall plants – the tough guys – into which the weaker climbers and creepers are allowed to scramble, gaining protection and support from their host plants. With some of the outstanding examples of wall plants listed below as your hardcore planting, and by introducing selected highlight plants, you can create a series of interesting and rewarding combinations, whatever the growing conditions.

Year-round interest: Some ivies, particularly *Hedera colchica* 'Sulphur Heart' and *H. helix* in variegated forms; *Lonicera japonica* 'Halliana'; *Cotoneaster horizontalis* and other cotoneasters; *Cytisus battandieri*.

CYTISUS BATTANDIERI

Winter specials: *Chaenomeles; Garrya elliptica; Jasminum nudiflorum; Camellia* x *williamsii*.
Spring specials: *Teucrium fruticans; Forsythia suspensa; Clematis montana*.
Summer and autumn specials: All climbing roses; honeysuckles; *Schizophragma integrifolium*; vines such as *Vitis vinifera* 'Purpurea'; *Clematis viticella* hybrids, *C.* x *jackmanii* hybrids; *Campsis radicans*.

Above: In this composition of climbing plants a potato vine (*Solanum crispum* 'Glasnevin') partners a large-flowered hybrid clematis, combining complementary colours and contrasting flower shapes. The container planted with trailing ground ivy (*Glechoma hederacea*) adds further interest.

USING CLIMBERS

As with 'wall plants', my definition of climbers is somewhat loose. Many will be natural scramblers, with or without the means to twine, to clutch with tendrils or to hold on with adventitious roots, and will be at home scrambling through their host plants. But there are others which are subsidiary plants, in that they would not be strong enough to act as supports for other climbers, and yet are not, technically speaking, climbers. One that springs to mind, *Coronilla*

valentina subsp. *glauca*, is a lax shrub, although perfect on a wall and of great value in a small garden because of its ability to flower almost constantly. But it is too weak to support much else growing among its pretty glaucous foliage.

Climbers, though using wall plants as their supports, must work in harmony with them, rather than eclipsing them completely. It is important to ensure that the planting is well balanced, with the most vigorous climbers restricted to growing among the most robust wall plants. It takes practice to get the balance right, but remedial action, on all but the most rampant of plants, is relatively simple in vertical gardening.

Some plants – be they wall plants or climbers – are better on their own, either because they look prettier when unencumbered, or because they grow better without any form of competition. Wisteria, though perfectly happy in a mix, can be more floriferous on its own, when the stems have had a chance to ripen in the sun without any other plants to shade them. But, apart from its cover of neutral foliage, wisteria is boring for much of the year and therefore benefits from summer-flowering plants nearby at least, if not actually intertwined. Many roses, though lovely in mixes, also look attractive displayed alone. As with everything in the garden, it is a question of balance.

PLANTING A SUNNY WALL

We shall assume, for this planting scenario in poor to reasonable soil, that summer temperatures are relatively high, with significant drops at night, but that in winter, though frost is prevalent in the area, the warm wall provides limited – but by no means total – protection. This wall is of greyish stone, though the colours of the flowers selected would go nearly as well with white, or with some shades of brick.

Warm-coloured wall plants could include the pineapple broom (*Cytisus battandieri*), not only for its mustard-yellow blooms but also for its silvery foliage.

Below: The blue-flowered wall plant *Ceanothus rigidus* makes a perfect host for the twining *Clematis macropetala* 'Pauline'; both flower in late spring.

GREAT TWISTERS & TWINERS

Composing vertical planting depends on your preferences, of course, and on the habitat to be planted, but below are some ideas for scrambling and twining plants to incorporate into a mixed wall-planting scheme.

RHODOCHITON ATROSANGUINEUS

Year-round interest: *Coronilla valentina* subsp. *glauca* 'Citrina'.

Winter and spring interest: *Clematis alpina*, *Clematis macropetala*.

Summer and autumn interest: *Lapageria rosea*; berberidopsis; sweet peas (*Lathyrus odoratus*); *Eccremocarpus scaber*; *Lophospermum erubescens*; *Cobaea scandens*; *Rhodochiton atrosanguineus*; *Tropaeolum speciosum*; *Tropaeolum* 'Ken Aslett'.

Climbers happy on their own: *Parthenocissus henryana*; *Parthenocissus tricuspidata*; *Plumbago auriculata*; wisteria.

Above: Though they need cool, shaded roots, climbing hydrangeas (*H. anomala* subsp. *petiolaris)* flower best if their stems grow into full light where the sun can ripen the wood to ensure a mass of lacecap blooms.

For more vivid colours, you could try *Fremontodendron californicum*, whose waxy, startling yellow flowers arrive in late spring and have a reprise in autumn. This is a hard plant to harmonize with others, because the hue of its flowers is so harsh, but it makes a gorgeous contrast with the purple flowers of *Abutilon* x *suntense*, itself vigorous enough to play the role of wall plant, and with the potato vine

(*Solanum crispum*) whose violet-blue flowers have yellow centres. I grow *Coronilla valentina* subsp. *glauca* at the base of my fremontodendron, partly to extend the yellow theme to the rest of the year, but also to provide a foliage contrast – blue-green against dark. For a gentler scheme, you could use the yellow *Rosa banksiae* 'Lutea', whose primrose flowers look lovely with the soft mauve-blue of wisteria.

In high summer, when a sunny part of the garden is inclined to overheat, cool foliage – or at least, the effect of cool foliage – can be helpful. Myrtle (*Myrtus communis*), whether freestanding or on a wall, has dark foliage of exactly the right note, as does ceanothus, whose intensely blue flowers, in late spring, would have blended to perfection with the Banksian rose, and with the fremontodendron.

Climbers to blend with these wall plants could include annual morning glories (*Ipomoea* – best started off under glass and planted out when the weather has warmed up) for their glorious blue flowers. *Lophospermum erubescens* – formerly *Maurandya* – has glowing purple-pink, foxglove-like blooms and pretty foliage. This will not scramble everywhere, but will drape the lower and mid-height sections of a wall with garlands of bloom from the second half of summer onwards. Other rapidly growing herbaceous plants which enjoy warm positions include *Cobaea scandens*, whose big purple or greenish-white bells are dotted rather than massed, and are followed by distinctive seedheads, and the extraordinary *Rhodochiton atrosanguineus*, which trails garlands of clove-shaped, almost black flowers, each under a little purplish-pink parachute-like calyx.

PLANTING AN EAST-FACING WALL

The classic wall for climbing roses is not especially hot but receives plenty of light and would have heavyish, alkaline soil. Any climbing rose is happy in such conditions, but here we might build up a pink theme using the thornless climber 'Zéphirine Drouhin' as the anchor plant, through which to pleach clematis in the blue to purple range. *Clematis* 'Jackmanii', common though it is, makes a superb companion for 'Zéphirine Drouhin', since its dark royal blue flowers harmonize perfectly with the plummy hue of the rose. You might be hard-pressed to find other climbers to add to such a fine combination but in the same area you could use *Chaenomeles* x *superba* for spring beauty, particularly the gorgeous 'Pink Lady' or, if you wanted a change in note, the brilliantly coloured 'Crimson and Gold' whose blood petals set off the golden stamens so well. An early-blooming clematis to work into the chaenomeles is *C. alpina* 'Helsingborg' – equally good with pink or blood red – which flowers for the last weeks of spring.

For a warmer theme, you could try the purple-leaved vine (*Vitis vinifera* 'Purpurea'), a superb foliage plant whose leaves run through a continuous series of changing colours from their silvery-sheened opening, through the dark wine-suffused summer period to autumn, when their colours deepen and intensify, making them as spectacular as many of the autumn flowers. Purple vine is good in conjunction with a red rose – 'Climbing Alec's Red' or the big, single-flowered 'Scarlet Fire'. The latter has the added advantage of vivid orange hips in autumn, which make a magnificent foil for the maturing vine foliage. As a final touch, the bluish-white *Clematis* 'Jackmanii Alba', less vigorous than other jackmanii hybrids, will gently thread its way through the foliage, picking up the blue tones of the vine leaves in its blue-cast petals.

PLANTING A WEST-FACING WALL

Warmer than east-facing, with a gentler contrast between day and night, a west-facing wall provides the best all-round conditions of any vertical structure. The nights are milder, day-time temperatures less extreme and there is no risk of damage by early sun on frost-laden plants. Such a wall or fence furnishes a superb site for warm, gentle colours on plants with

luxurious growth. Honeysuckles, particularly *Lonicera periclymenum*, love such conditions, flowering for months on end, often producing their final blooms as the berries ripen in autumn. For fragrance it is fine on its own but, blended with summer jasmine, the cocktail is heady! The cream to yellow blooms, particularly on such forms as 'Graham Thomas' or, with a dash of dusky red on the outsides of the petals, 'Serotina', associate well with the medium-flowered clematis 'Madame Julia Correvon' and the buff-yellow rose 'Gloire de Dijon'.

Left: This sunny corner, backed by a high wall, is made fragrant with roses and lavender, creating an ideal location for a seat.

Plants which naturally inhabit the trees of open woodland thrive in these conditions. Those that blend leafiness with flower, such as the climbing hydrangea (*H. anomala* subsp. *petiolaris*), are superb wall plants through which to weave other climbers. *Schizophragma integrifolium*, happier on its own, is a hydrangea relative with magnificent creamy-white blooms, forming bold lacecaps, each edged with oblong sterile florets.

USING VERTICAL STRUCTURES

Right: Wisteria is perfect for use on an arch because the blossoms hang so gracefully below the foliage. Besides the common blue *Wisteria sinensis* there are several white forms such as *W. japonica* 'Alba' (illustrated here) and a white species, *W. venusta*.

Walls and fences are only part of the vertical gardening story. Much of the interest, particularly in small gardens, comes from other upright structures, whether they be pergolas, arches or feature pillars or obelisks in borders.

GROWING CLIMBERS INTO TREES

When choosing a good combination, it is important to match the climber to the host plant, not only for artistic harmony, but also to ensure that the climber does not threaten to swamp the host, and that the tree or shrub is small enough for the climber not to be lost in its branches. *Clematis viticella* is a European species that has given rise to some superlative garden hybrids,

with small to medium-sized flowers produced in profusion in the second half of summer. These might almost have been created to thread into conifers, for their soft, deep colours of purple, blue or maroon are brought out by conifer leaves, particularly those with blue or gold foliage. The cultivar 'Minuet', with its white-centred purple blooms, or perhaps the starker white 'Alba Luxurians', contrasts well with the grey-green of prostrate junipers like *Juniperus prostratus* 'Grey Owl', for a low display, or can be persuaded to climb up taller upright ones, perhaps even the long, thin 'Skyrocket', where a purple or white garland can look so effective. The great advantage with forms of *Clematis viticella* is that they can be cut back as hard as you like, in autumn or late winter, to leave the host plant uncluttered, to be enjoyed at its own time of beauty. The same plants can be used with delightful results in evergreens such as laurels or hollies.

If you happen to have an evergreen hedge whose base is shaded but whose upper zone is in sun, try planting *Tropaeolum speciosum*, a South American climber of modest vigour that loves to have its feet in the cool and its head in the sun. It will highlight sombre evergreens with explosions of vivid scarlet blooms. If the soil is moist and leafy, *T. speciosum* will seed around until a sizeable colony has formed.

MAN-MADE SUPPORTS

Useful though host plants are, without them it is still a simple matter to increase your garden's content of vertical displays. There is an extensive choice of manufactured climbing supports suitable for the small garden, from arch systems in wrought iron to simple frames made of withy hurdles, which will suit most styles of garden. In formal plantings, simplicity is the key, so that a trellis obelisk, for example, needs nothing more than a single clematis, perhaps backed by decorative foliage. If the obelisk is big enough, the classic combination of golden hop (*Humulus lupulus* 'Aureus') and *Clematis* 'Etoile Violette' is perfect, or a

simple planting of sweet peas, preferably in a single colour, might do as well.

A single pillar rose on a straight oak post will make a useful vertical statement if you limit its leading shoots to a maximum of three or four, with the top pinched out and the stems flexed or twisted, so that the flowers develop along their length. If you use moderately vigorous varieties, such as the apricot 'Claire Jacquier' or the cream 'Alister Stella Gray', you will need to discipline them to keep them in shape, but their thick, lush growth will give a very different effect from more restrained climbers such as 'Danse du Feu' or 'Golden Showers'. With these, as with the gloriously fragrant, pink Damask rose, 'Ispahan', there

will be less exuberant growth but still plenty of colour and form for summer.

On pergolas or larger structures, it is important not only to ensure that there is rich companion planting, but also to address the problems of the quieter seasons. Consider stalwarts like Japanese honeysuckle for autumn fragrance, winter jasmine for short-day colour and, if there is space, the huge-leaved, rampant evergreen *Clematis armandii* for its winter foliage. Wisterias are wonderful when hanging above your head across a pergola, but they can make for a boring, leafy tunnel for the rest of summer, once they have flowered; their gnarled and twisted trunks, glorious in winter in old age, are rather nondescript when young.

Above: An arch in a high brick wall is planted with a mix of climbing roses and clematis. In full bloom is the large-flowered clematis hybrid, 'H.F. Young'. Old shrub roses in the foreground help to create a seamless join between the ground and the wall in this informal scene.

CLOTHING THE VERTICAL SPACE

Many climbing plants reach a climax of beauty before their leaves fall and growth comes to an end. In this autumn picture foliage and fruit figure as strongly as does flower, but the late-flowering clematis 'Bill Mackenzie' still provides yellow blooms among its fluffy seedheads and the last of the rose blooms ('Gloire de Dijon' and 'Ena Harkness') are hanging on. The foliage of the purple-leaved vine is enhanced to rich ruby red, making a fine contrast with the clematis 'Etoile Rose'. Most of these wall plants will thrive in reasonable soil, especially if it is enriched each year and mulched to keep the roots cool.

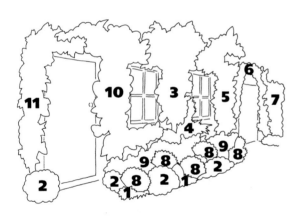

THE PLANTS

1 *Erysimum* 'Bowles Mauve'

2 *Geranium* x *oxonianum* 'Wargrave Pink'

3 *Rosa* 'Ena Harkness'

4 *Jasminum nudiflorum*

5 *Rosa* 'Gloire de Dijon'

6 *Clematis* 'Etoile Rose'

7 *Vitis vinifera* 'Purpurea'

8 *Festuca glauca*

9 *Dianthus* 'Doris'

10 *Lonicera* x *tellmanniana*

11 *Clematis* 'Bill Mackenzie'

GREAT CONTAINER PLANTS

Containers transform a garden. By changing emphasis, perhaps with nothing more than a single urn or pot, you can alter an entire view. A small group of containers will bring colour and shape to an otherwise dull corner or enable you to arrange a collection of your favourite plants to their best advantage. Containers also help to create highlights within borders or they can be used as focal points at the end of a short or long vista; they can furnish garden entrances or doors or they can be used to distract attention from unsightly objects. Even if you have no soil – a roof garden or balcony, perhaps, or just a small, paved yard – containers will enable you to convert even the most unforgiving space into a small garden that is both authentic and enjoyable.

The other great advantages of containers are that they are mobile and extremely versatile, making their uses numerous, particularly in small spaces. Most containers are small enough to be shifted by hand, enabling you to relocate and rearrange them as you want; with the help of webbing straps and barrows, it is far easier to move even large pots, with their plants intact, than it is to dig up and re-plant mature shrubs or trees. In a very restricted space, their mobility allows you to ring the changes whenever you want, bringing in containers that look their best to replace those that are on the wane.

You can grow practically anything in a container. Tropical plants, for example, can be displayed in containers outdoors in summer, even in cold climates, provided they are taken indoors for winter protection. Winter foliage displays can be replaced by summer flowers, instantly, without having to wait for them to establish. Containers can also be used to provide special conditions for plants that would not be happy in your natural garden soil. Camellias, for example, abhor my limestone soil but are happy growing in peat-based ericaceous compost in pots on my terrace. A great many spring bulbs do better in containers than anywhere else: if planted deeply enough, bulbs in containers can be left to their own devices and will flower year after year.

Above: Certain plants are almost maintenance-free and therefore ideal for containers. The sempervirens in this terracotta pan require minimal watering and yet provide perennial interest.

Opposite: Though one associates them with wide, open spaces, grasses make surprisingly good container subjects. With their arching leaves and their gentle movement in the breeze, they are as ornamental as any flowering subject.

Above: Permanent container plants must provide year-round interest. This Japanese maple, *Acer palmatum* 'Dissectum Purpureum', loses its lacy foliage in winter but makes a beautiful silhouette with its naked branches.

Right: The container itself – a beautiful amphora – is the main focus in this scene. The succulent planted in its top has been chosen to set off the pot to perfection.

CHOOSING THE RIGHT PLANTS

Although almost any species is reasonably happy in a container, certain plants lend themselves to pots, troughs or urns far more readily than others. Among shrubs or trees, those whose growth rate is modest and whose root systems are compact will adapt best. Dwarf maples, for example, are superlative container plants, achieving a venerable aged appearance, with branches and trunks that thicken and gnarl far more quickly than if the trees had been planted in open ground. *Acer palmatum*, in almost any of its forms, gives a Japanese or oriental feel that is particularly noticeable in such named varieties as 'Dissectum Atropurpureum', 'Bloodgood', with its near black stems, or 'Burgundy Lace' with its gorgeously coloured, almost filigree foliage. Camellias are adaptable to containers, though they keep far smaller and more compact than in open ground, and the more dwarf rhododendron species, such as *R. yakushimanum*, are superb in containers, provided they are never – but never – allowed to dry out. Among evergreens, the versatile and good-natured hollies (*Ilex*) make terrific container plants, happy with their roots restricted as long as the tops are trimmed to a size that can easily be maintained by the root system.

Any good herbaceous container plant should suffer the indignity of transplanting with minimal side effects. One of the reasons for using containers is to be able to make fairly profound planting changes quickly, often during the growing season. Plants that resent disturbance are therefore hardly suitable for mixed containers, though they are fine on their own; most woody plants, for example, are best undisturbed, except during their dormant period.

The extensive repertoire of tender plants, both annuals and perennials, that has been developed for summer bedding seems to be made for containers and will often put up with the most brutal transplanting, even in midsummer. Lobelias, pelargoniums, petunias, pansies and diascias, as long as their roots do not dry out, will tolerate transplanting at almost any time. Plants that are easily grown from cuttings will always be desirable container subjects, especially in the rush of summer work. *Argyranthemum frutescens*, *Nemesia caerulea*, *Osteospermum* species and *Felicia amelloides* are all examples of plants that can sometimes be rooted, at the height of the growing season, simply by breaking young shoots off and pushing them into the compost of the container. That has to be a bonus!

Sustained interest is an essential quality of plants for successful container use, particularly during the summer when you are likely to spend the most time outdoors. Window boxes and hanging baskets, in particular, are only good when every plant is giving the maximum in terms of display, with plenty of potential to carry the flowering through to the very end of the growing season. These requirements are not difficult to meet, provided you select the right species – and the right varieties – and observe an unbroken pattern of feeding and watering. Plants that will give value in a year-round planting scheme include ivies, *Lamium maculatum*, *Euphorbia myrsinites*, epimediums, dwarf conifers and trailing kinds of euonymus.

Containers have almost as much potential for winter and spring use as for summer, and the same principles apply. There is no room for passengers, so plants which will provide winter interest before developing into their spring display will be preferable to those whose winter appearance is dispiriting. We will look at ideas for winter and spring cocktails on pages 98–99, but the best examples of plants which provide constant interest for these minor seasons would include winter pansies (*Viola*), such as the 'Universal' series which bloom sporadically during winter but have a magnificent spring flourish before wearing themselves out with flowering. Winter heathers also provide months of clean, bright colours, particularly

the white and pale pink forms of *Erica carnea* and the hybrid *E.* x *darleyensis*. Being evergreen, they provide considerable interest even when they are not flowering, but varieties such as *E. carnea* 'Springwood White' and 'Springwood Pink' bloom for so long that it would be hard to find a reason for not including them in a collection of winter containers.

Above: Hydrangeas always look handsome in pots. Here, *Hydrangea* 'Blue Wave' creates a feature in a border, where the pale terracotta pot is set off by the shapely hosta leaves.

SEASONAL PLANTING IDEAS

The most popular way of using containers is to accommodate a burgeoning mix of rapidly growing summer plants, many of them tender and most purchased each year from nurseries and garden centres for the annual ritual of planting out. A high proportion of these plants – although considered annuals and therefore discarded at the end of the summer – are, in fact, perennial and can be overwintered for use in later years as well as being easy to propagate. Even petunias, lobelia and most salvias will grow from cuttings raised by the same method as used for the more frequently overwintered fuchsias and pelargoniums.

TEMPORARY SUMMER SCHEMES

It is worth giving consideration to the nature of summer containers and considering alternatives to the more usual, somewhat hackneyed planting recipes for basket, pot and window box based around ivy-leaved pelargoniums and trailing fuchsias. Pelargoniums come in such a bewildering variety of shapes, sizes, colours and habits that one wonders why commercial breeders insist on introducing so many new varieties, each one more garish and unnatural-looking than its predecessor. Many of them are in fact more suitable for tray production – bred to look enticing at the plant centre – rather than to last all season in the garden. And yet so many of the earlier varieties and of the original species are ideal for small private gardens. While seed-raised cultivars of pelargoniums often run to seed far too quickly in a garden and must be constantly dead-headed to stimulate new blooms, those raised from cuttings, while they may be more laborious to reproduce, are often much more rewarding in a garden, where their foliage effects are as impressive as their flowers. The stocky, variegated cultivar 'Frank Headley', for example, is an immensely valuable foliage plant for container use and has the bonus of single blooms in soft salmon orange, produced in modest sprays. It makes a perfect companion for dark foliage and flowers – perhaps those of deep purple heliotrope or such other pelargoniums as the equally compact, red-flowered, dark bronze-leaved 'Friesdorf'.

The daisy tribe, Asteraceae, makes a huge contribution in summer, many of the species flowering continuously throughout the growing season. As an alternative to the usual gaudy flower and foliage mix, last summer I planted two large rough-glazed pots with a mixture of the South African *Felicia amelloides* 'Santa Anita', whose small, yellow-eyed blue daisies made a misty, meadow-like effect, blended evenly with the similar-sized flowers of *Rhodanthemum gayanum*, pink with a chocolate-brown centre. Not only was the colour combination pleasant, but the soft, understated effect was natural and relaxed, perfect for my country garden, and the display lasted throughout the summer and deep into autumn.

Single plantings are lovely too, especially on sites where the choice of colour is crucial. The 'Balcon series' of *Pelargonium*, raised in Europe, look delightful in hanging baskets on their own, where in time they create huge misty globes of vivid red, in the case of 'Roi des Balcons Impérial', and soft, rather washy pink in 'Hederinum. If mixed with anything at all, one other species – perhaps the trailing foliage of *Helichrysum petiolare* – can be added to soften the outline and enhance the colour by providing a silvery contrast. For summer foliage plants in hanging baskets or window boxes, one of the most ravishing species is *Lotus berthelotii*, which comes from the Atlantic island of Tenerife. This member of the pea family has foliage that is so pale a grey and so finely divided that it looks almost like silver filigree. But the plant's crowning glory is its flower – a crimson, sharp-pointed 'beak' that appears along mature stems. Though often used as background for its foliage, this plant is spectacular enough to grow entirely alone.

Right: This amazingly rich and varied summer planting is virtually all done with containerized plants. Using large pots and tubs has resulted in growth so strong that many of the containers have disappeared among the greenery. Plants of note include the dramatic foliage plant *Melianthus major;* closer to ground level is a mix of heliotrope, violas, verbenas and marguerite daisies. White nicotianas provide evening fragrance and, to follow, there will be lilies in abundance.

Above: The mobility of containers allows them to be placed to create informal or formal groups. The topiary birds add a note of wit: this form of topiary can be achieved speedily by training a small-leaved evergreen climber such as ivy over a pre-shaped wire frame.

PERMANENT SUMMER PLANTING

Lavenders, santolina and artemisia all make useful permanent subjects for summer containers; they look especially pretty placed near roses, where their silvery foliage sets off the flower colours so well. With penstemons planted among their silver foliage – with or without roses – and with repeat-flowering border pinks such as 'Diane', 'Haytor' or 'Doris', a long flowering period is assured.

The compact 'Patio' varieties of repeat-flowering rose are best for container use. For vigour the plummy-pink 'Chatsworth' takes some beating although it is less gentle in its colouring than the softer pink of 'Little Bo Peep' or the slightly deeper 'Pretty Polly'. Some Patio roses are eye-wateringly garish, but 'Sweet Magic' manages to achieve a warm gold, well set off by shiny foliage, without your needing sunglasses to sit near it. Among modern hybrids, disease can be problematic, particularly black spot and mildew, but a variety that claims total resistance is 'Flower Carpet', a rather strident pink, cluster-flowered rose whose semi-trailing habit lets it double as ground cover.

In semi-shade, hostas make first-rate summer container plants, creating a more muted display which relies on different foliage for its colour effects. In gardens where slugs are troublesome, containers may be the only way to grow hostas without holes in their foliage; standing the pots on sharp grit and making sure the leaves are not in contact with the ground will help to prevent slug attack. Other rewarding container subjects for part-shade include grasses, such as *Hakonechloa*, busy lizzies (*Impatiens*), ferns like athyrium, polystichum and asplenium, as well as such spring-flowering shrubs as camellias, azaleas and dwarf rhododendrons.

SPRING PLANTING IDEAS

Most temporary container plants that look magnificent in spring can be short on colour and style for winter. All-time favourites such as the wallflowers (*Cheiranthus cheiri*), for example, can be dreary in midwinter, as can forget-me-nots (*Myosotis*). And yet, as the days begin to lengthen, the fragrance of freshly opened wallflowers, and the sight of their warming colours, contrasted with the clean blue of forget-me-nots, is one of the most cheering events of the spring. The solution is to use them in moderation. In a small garden there is much to gain by planting up some containers with, say, yellow or red wallflowers (I love the glowing, deep red 'Vulcan') and bordering these with *Myosotis* 'Blue Ball' or perhaps with button daisies (*Bellis perennis*). In a winter container, you can enhance the drabness of the foliage with winter bulbs. Half a dozen aconite blooms, a handful of *Crocus chrysanthus*, the Italian *C. imperati* or a small botanical tulip such as *T. pulchella* – or indeed several or all of these – will provide welcome sparks of interest during the bleak months. If their dying foliage gets in the way after the flowers have faded, you can carefully remove the whole plants and replant them in a border for future years, making room for replacement planting in the container.

Wallflowers beg to be underplanted with hybrid tulips for the main spring display and this can produce some ravishing combinations. Red tulips with orange or yellow wallflowers, for instance, make a strident show, but the dark tulip 'Queen of the Night' with pale plum or ivory wallflowers makes a more subtle partnership. Yellow tulips such as 'Bellona' or 'West Point' or late pink ones like 'Clara Butt' or 'Ballade' are gorgeous with blue forget-me-nots. The little narcissus, 'Hawera', a butter-yellow Triandrus hybrid, has become popular as a tulip accompaniment and it is very much at home with grape hyacinths (*Muscari*) too. When planting all these in containers you can afford to plant the bulbs thickly for maximum effect. Even if they are almost touching, they will still produce healthy flowers, massed together for impact.

Though more often associated with meadow or woodland planting, many primulas are superb in containers, either alone or in the company of other spring beauties. A highly collectible old variety is a polyanthus type called 'Guinevere'. Raised in Ireland, this has dark, almost bronze foliage, coppery-red stems and contrasting pale lilac flowers. It makes a delicious harmony with lemon, cream or white flowers; it also looks pretty associated with blue and would make a fitting companion to hyacinths in any colour but pink.

Another group of primulas underestimated for use in containers are the auriculas. *Primula auricula* inhabits dry semi-shade in the wild and makes a natural container subject. It can bloom from mid-spring until the beginning of summer and elevating it above ground level allows you to enjoy its clean, delicate fragrance. There is a wide range of flower colours and certain named varieties are especially gorgeous: 'Old Irish Blue' is like the faded velvet of a Madonna's gown; 'Chorister' is mustard-yellow with a white collar and 'Old Red Dusty Miller' needs no description.

IDEAS FOR WINTER CONTAINERS

Although one is hardly likely to linger in a garden in winter, an empty container is a depressing sight. It reproaches you as you peer through the window or walk past in a desolate, frosty garden. But there are

some delightful plants with evergreen foliage and winter flower to assemble for a cheering winter display. Winter colour also comes from little bulbs, such as aconites and spring snowflake (*Leucojum vernum*), as well as violas or pansies which can be in bloom, sporadically, all winter.

For my own garden in winter I planted up a half-barrel using one of my favourite colour combinations, bronze or purple with blue-green or grey. It contains the Mediterranean, prostrate *Euphorbia myrsinites*, with its curious blue-green scaly foliage and S-shaped stems which hang, albeit a little awkwardly, over the side. Behind this and offsetting it is the broader, leathery foliage of *Bergenia purpurascens*, whose normally greenish leaves become deeply burnished by frost in winter, and whose startling pink flowers are a useful bonus at winter's end. For more long-term winter bloom, I included the winter heather, *Erica carnea* 'Springwood White'.

Above: A fine winter container is planted with *Bergenia cordifolia*, whose leaves are touched with bronze in cold weather, and a drought- and frost-resistant fern. Underplanting these evergreens with tulips produces a beautiful spring flourish.

BALCONY AND ROOF GARDENS

A balcony or roof garden may only be made possible through the use of containers. Even if there are beds and borders, these are likely to be shallow and should therefore be treated much like containers. There may well be weight restrictions on a roof or balcony too, and limitations on how liberally you can throw water about on the top of a flat building. In spite of all the constraints, it is feasible to make a beautiful and luxuriant garden out of almost nothing, even though

every bag of compost has to be carted upstairs. These gardens usually have special needs too. Balcony gardens, if they face the sun for most of the day, will irritatingly have all their flowers pointing away from you. Where light is restricted, the plants will all lean in the same direction, unless you are clever with the way you arrange them. A good ruse is to place as many as possible at the back of the balcony, furthest from the edge, to be enjoyed when you are sitting outside.

Climbers come into their own here, since the vertical dimensions of a balcony are likely to be larger than the floor space. Place the containers against a wall so the climbers have some support, or train them to climb and tumble over the railings. If the habitat is warm, you might be able to invest in some special climbers to give extra colour and fragrance. *Trachelospermum jasminoides*, for example, is a slightly tender relative of jasmine, with creamy-white flowers in summer and an enchanting fragrance. In a reliably frost-free location, you might even try bougainvillea on a balcony, since it survives with very little water.

On a shaded balcony you are likely to limit yourself to plants suited to cooler climates, including such less vigorous climbers as the beautiful, shade-loving *Lapageria rosea* or, in a cold region, variegated-leaved ivies. Though naturally vigorous, most of these will behave themselves if their roots are contained. The large-leaved *Hedera canariensis* is useful, especially 'Gloire de Marengo', but for a more frost-prone position, use a variegated or green-leaved form of English ivy (*Hedera helix*); 'Adam' has nicely marked silver-grey and green foliage, 'Ivalace' has prettily ruffled leaves and in 'Heron' the leaves are thin and angular, like the bird's foot.

Small trees, or shrubs trimmed into topiary shapes, will give your roof garden or balcony an outline planting, while keeping everything in scale. Their strategic placing could help to blot out eyesores on an urban landscape. Almost any species that enjoys being clipped when grown in open ground will be as happy

Left: An interesting selection of container-grown evergreen and foliage plants, including *Heuchera micrantha*, hostas and a pot-grown fig, make this roof garden delightful to look at and shelter it from the worst of the weather. A climbing rose grown against the trellis contributes summer flowers and scent.

Right: Generous containers and stark white trelliswork give this elevated garden a formal feel which is softened by the natural growth of plants, which include *Fatsia japonica*, topiary box and a rhododendron.

Opposite: A combination of temporary and permanent planting gives this small yard a sense of continuity, but with changes through the year. Ivy on the trellis forms a permanent background in front of which sweet peas and runner beans trained on bamboo 'wigwams' make a fragrant, colourful and productive summer display.

in a pot, but box (*Buxus sempervirens*), myrtle (*Myrtus communis*), dwarf conifers, the low-growing species of laurel (*Prunus laurocerasus*) and *Euonymus radicans* are especially useful for containers.

Where it is possible to protect plants from frost, you could try forms of *Citrus* – particularly lemons – as specimen container trees. Their blossoms will bring late-winter and spring fragrance and the aromatic fruit is highly decorative. Other citrus include small orange trees – amenable to topiary – and kumquats, whose small oval fruits are almost too pretty to pick.

In areas where wind can be troublesome, avoid brittle-stemmed plants and make wider use of such

low-growing plants as verbenas, *Osteospermum ecklonis prostratum*, *Convolvulus sabatius* and trailing pelargoniums. The best container plants for screening are bush and hedge species of holly, osmanthus, aucuba, elaeagnus, *Fuchsia magellanica*, camellia and evergreen cotoneaster. Make the most of herbaceous or annual climbers such as clematis, *Cobaea scandens*, golden hop (*Humulus lupulus* 'Aureus') and honeysuckle for summer interest and scent, as well as winter jasmine (*Jasminum nudiflorum*), honeysuckle and ivy.

A CONTAINED GARDEN

Imagine a small area surrounded by high walls, with a paved surface and no natural soil whatsoever. It may sound daunting but is in fact a perfect location in which to create a container garden. All the usual planting principles apply, the outline being provided by a small number of generous-sized pots planted with evergreen trees or shrubs. Camellias will thrive here or, for a more erect shape, try conifers, bay or even *Magnolia grandiflora*, which has been trained and clipped into a column. A line of container-grown yuccas along the back wall provides an eye-catching feature in this enclosed garden.

Raised beds enable plants with more questing roots, such as climbers, to thrive; trailing plants such as lobelia and felicia can be planted to cascade over the low wall, softening its edges. Raised platforms or benches would provide an opportunity to develop collections of much smaller plants to be grown in pots or pans and enjoyed closer to eye level. One of the joys of containers is that you can cheat, almost regardless of season, bringing in new plants and discarding unwanted ones more or less at will. Large summer bulbs, such as agapanthus or lilies, make a wonderful temporary display and, if conditions are mild, you can even enjoy exotic orchids outside.

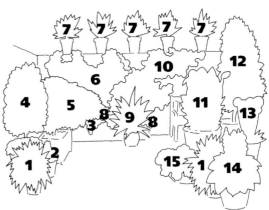

THE PLANTS

1   *Hakonechloa macra*
    'Aureola'

2   Yellow orchid

3   *Lobelia richardsonii*

4   *Camellia japonica*

5   *Acer palmatum*
    'Dissectum
    Atropurpureum'

6   *Clematis* 'Etoile
    Violette'

7   *Yucca filamentosa*

8   *Felicia amelloides*

9   *Cordyline australis*
    'Purpurea Group'

10 *Humulus lupulus*
    'Aureus'

11 *Lilium martagon*

12 *Laurus nobilis*

13 *Agapanthus*
    'Headbourne Hybrids'

14 *Hosta sieboldiana*

15 *Euphorbia myrsinites*

GREAT PLANTS FOR PROBLEM PLACES

As we all know, the ideal garden has perfect soil, is probably situated in a beneficial microclimate and will have been planted at least fifty years previously to provide efficient and decorative shelter from all climatic extremes. In design and layout, it exhibits the right combination of well-lit and gently shaded areas so that the widest possible combination of plants can be enjoyed. There are no pests in the dream garden, and storms, blizzards and heatwaves are, of course, unheard of.

If only life were like that! In reality, almost everyone's garden has a 'no-go' area where soil is blighted or where conditions are so gloomy or so dry that practically nothing will grow. Country gardens, especially where the owners have gone out of their way to preserve the rural view, are often too exposed and windy for any but the toughest plants. In cities, where dwellings are crowded cheek by jowl, privacy may only be possible by erecting high walls, screens and fences, which block out sunshine as well as alien eyes. Local authorities, in their efforts to keep urban areas as green and alive as possible, encourage the planting of trees in the streets, and often preserve unwanted trees in private gardens by enforcement, creating more shade and causing undesirably dry conditions at their roots. What is to be done about the garden, in such conditions? Indeed, is it possible to garden a blighted site at all?

Positive thinking dictates that it is. Plants of one kind or another will grow practically anywhere and there is a small but useful hardcore of dependable plants that will tolerate even the most adverse growing conditions. It may not be feasible to achieve perfection in a problem garden but, with appropriate action taken to alleviate the constraints set by the growing conditions, and with a judicious selection of plants that will tolerate the adversity, you can achieve results that will surprise and delight you.

Above: *Anemone blanda*, a Mediterranean native, flourishes in free-draining gravel in dry shade.

Opposite: A difficult, dry corner of a garden is transformed simply by selecting the right plants. *Artemisia stelleriana* provides a silvery foreground backed by dark-leaved sedums, grasses and the mauve onion relative, *Tulbaghia violacea*.

105

REDUCING THE PROBLEMS

Obvious though it may seem, the best starting point is to understand your particular problem. In an existing garden, the signs of difficulty are usually – but not always – manifest. In heavy shade, all the plants look drawn up and hungry, with too little foliage and too much stem. In exposed gardens, you can often tell which side the wind comes from simply by looking at trees and shrubs, many of which will have developed a decided bias to leeward. Strongly alkaline soil will produce a yellowing of the foliage in some plants, especially early in the growing season, and these will

Below: Shade is one of the most common garden problems. Much can be done to alleviate the difficulty by selecting, as here, plants with subtle variations in leaf colour and texture, and by using pale-coloured or white flowers.

often scorch in direct sunlight, making matters worse. Waterlogging can result in sinister fungal growths on lawns, can make trees or shrubs languish and die, particularly during wet periods, and will cause some soils to turn heavy and sour.

You may want to invest in professional advice at the development stage of your garden. It also makes sense to know exactly what kind of soil you have and what deficiencies it may exhibit. Most people like to measure pH (a means of assessing the acidity or alkalinity of the soil) and will then restrict themselves to plants that are suited to the soil type. But if you are not technically minded and do not want to go to the trouble of testing, it can be almost as reliable to look around your neighbourhood and see which plants are thriving, which look sorry for themselves, and to note any obvious absences. You do not need an expert to tell you that heavy clay soil sticks to your shoes, whereas free-draining sand will be easy to work on soon after even the heaviest of rains or that, whereas the former will retain its moisture practically for ever, the latter is likely to dry out too soon and push your plants into a state of stress associated with drought. While a professional horticulturist will be able to give you an assessment of what is wrong, there is nothing like living with a problem garden to get to the bottom of your trouble. It may take a season or more of trial and error, but part of the fun of gardening is getting to know all the quirks and flaws that are special to your own plot, then achieving mastery over them.

Once you have given the whole garden a thorough check-up and identified the major problems, the next step, before any serious planting begins, is to do all you can to alleviate the difficulties. The problem areas are likely to fall into one of the following categories.

DRY SHADE This is just about the worst problem of all. Walls, especially old ones, not only throw shadow but can sometimes act like candle-wicks, drawing moisture out of the soil by capillary action and evaporating it through their surface. This capillary effect is accelerated in warm weather. Large trees are even worse because they hog all the moisture from the ground and then keep the rain off with their canopy of foliage. You cannot demolish walls but you can paint their surfaces white or a pale colour – this helps to reflect more light and relieve the gloom, although it also tends to reduce the leavening effect of white or pale-coloured flowers. Trees are easier to deal with than walls: by thinning out their crowns and pruning with care you can reduce the density of the canopy and thus admit more light down to ground level.

DAMP SHADE To a keen plantsperson this is hardly a problem, since such a wealth of moisture-loving plants are also happiest in low light levels. But where shade is too dense, flowering and growth will be impaired, even of plants that naturally inhabit the deepest woodland. Consider creating new contours, sinking a hole, or holes, for ponds or water features and raising other areas into mounds, banks, steps or terraces for plants which require better drainage. As with dry shade, try to thin the foliage canopy of trees by strategic pruning of their overhanging branches.

DRY POSITION Use moisture-retaining mulches each year and work plenty of compost or organic material into the ground. Not only will this remedial action help to conserve water, but it will also improve the structure and, ultimately, the fertility of your soil. If you have to use water, be sure to use it efficiently, soaking the ground at night or in the early morning, when evaporation is reduced.

WINDY AND EXPOSED POSITION The solution to weather problems is simple: create a shelter. Whether integrated as part of the design, or simply erected as a temporary measure, while sheltering plants get them-selves established, some means to reduce the force of the wind is essential. Shrubs, hedges and trees are

more effective, and cheaper, than walls or solid wooden fences, because they slow down the rate of the wind rather than blocking it off completely, causing swirls and eddy currents which can be more damaging than a steady gale. Living screens usually look better than man-made ones because they create a natural-looking background to the choice garden plants.

POOR SOIL Good drainage is especially important on heavy or clay soils. It can be improved by installing a drainage system and by incorporating plenty of coarse fibrous material into the top 15–30cm (6–12in) of soil. Grit, gravel and sand can also alleviate a heavy soil structure if mixed in while digging. Soil structure is fragile and can be ruined by too much compaction, so avoid working with wet soils and think twice before walking on beds and borders – your own weight could compact the structure. Encourage your plants to develop into a thick cover as fast as possible, since they themselves actually improve the soil, shad-ing it with their foliage and feeding it with leaves that fall off and rot. Soil improvement is not an overnight task: it is part of the regular routine work and will continue for as long as you garden.

Above: A hot dry garden with plenty of greenery and strong colours, which come from a wise choice of drought-resistant plants. Sun roses (*Helianthemum*) give long-lasting colour even in the driest soil; besides the red variety in the foreground, they come in a range of colours including pink, yellow and orange.

PLANTS FOR DRY SHADE

Once you have done everything you can to alleviate the problems in a shady garden, the best results will always depend on a careful choice of plants. With the right selection of species, it is possible to create interest and beauty in dry, shady places, even where you might have thought that nothing would grow.

THE OUTLINE

It may be desirable, from an aesthetic point of view, to create a strong profile with a tree or trees or a selection of shrubs, but if your outline plants are too tall and too spreading, this will add to the difficulties of dry shade. Fastigiate trees – those which grow like exclamation marks, with erect branches – cause minimal shading and can be very effective. The erect cherry, *Prunus* 'Umineko', has the added advantage of stark white blossoms in spring, but its display is brief compared to the constant interest of the female holly, *Ilex* 'Green Pillar'. Without clipping or trimming, this forms a dense bottle-green pillar, decorated in winter with brilliant red berries. Other shade-tolerant hollies are those with variegated foliage, one of the toughest of which is *I. aquifolium* 'Silver Queen' (a male, despite its name) and therefore perfect for pollinating the female 'Green Pillar'. If you plan to introduce any new deciduous trees to an already shaded planting, select those which are latest to come into leaf, or whose leaf cover is least dense. *Robinia pseudoacacia*, for example, seldom comes to life before late spring and yet is quite quick to lose its leaves in autumn. It also has a graceful, open habit and therefore throws relatively gentle shade.

Among evergreen shrubs the choice is wide, but the number of dull, green nonentities that merely exist, rather than rejoicing in life, is large and many are best avoided – it is better to have bare soil than a half-dead plant! Avoid the dreary clones of *Aucuba japonica*, some of which can look horribly bilious in poor light – selecting, rather, those whose foliage is bright or a good, green-leaved female that will berry freely. For vivid colour, *A. japonica* 'Picturata' is positively startling, for its foliage carries bold golden splashes and, being male, it will pollinate the variety 'Salicifolia', a prolific female with narrow plain green leaves and stems which are sea-green. If you want a more formal appearance, *Osmanthus delavayi* is a fine evergreen which flowers fragrantly in spring and lends itself to clipping. The pure white waxy flowers, though not large, are showy enough to stand out, particularly where sunlight is at a premium.

Almost everyone grows mahonia in shade and, in spite of the introduction of several named hybrids and cultivars, the hardiest, the most fragrant and, in my view, easily the most handsome is *M. japonica*. The racemes of flowers are more sinuous than in other species and a wonderfully gentle primrose-yellow, smelling strongly of lily-of-the-valley. In mild districts an alternative is the taller, more erect *M. lomariifolia* whose mustard-yellow flowers are more perky, but the naked trunks are less alluring. Certain hydrangeas can be surprisingly tolerant of dense shade and, though they flower less readily, will still produce smaller, lighter mopheads or lacecaps. Extremes of dryness, however, will discourage them to such an extent that their appearance detracts from, rather than enhances, the garden. In such conditions, you could try, as an alternative, that odd inter-generic hybrid x *Fatshedera lizei* for its bold, ivy-like foliage.

THE UNDERSTOREY

At the feet of such shrubs, you could raise a mix of woodland plants which, in the wild, are used to dry, cool conditions once the overshadowing trees come into leaf. Even if the soil is too parched for primroses and violets, you can persevere with the fascinating range of epimediums: *Epimedium rubrum* and *E.*

alpinum are especially good where moisture is short. *Hepatica transsilvanica* is surprisingly drought-tolerant too, as is the clump-forming butcher's broom (*Ruscus aculeatus*). The stinking iris (*I. foetidissima*) provides constant green, sword-like foliage and quietly pretty violet blooms in early summer and sports dramatic orange seeds which adhere to the parchment-coloured pods as they split and gape in late autumn.

Among spring flowers, the most fragrant for dry shade is lily-of-the-valley (*Convallaria majalis*), which is available in a dusky pink form, 'Rosea', as well as the more familiar white. Both these make excellent companions to the taller Solomon's seal (*Polygonatum*), forming a useful leaf cover later in the year. Certain species of violet will, just about, tolerate dry shade: the dog violet (*Viola riviniana*) is probably the easiest to maintain – but watch out for its capacity to seed itself absolutely everywhere – and *V. labradorica* the most handsome, less for its blue flowers than for its dark purple foliage. A recently introduced plant with superb dark foliage is *Euphorbia dulcis* 'Chameleon'.

Left: In dry shade, epimediums like *E. rubrum* give a changing run of colour, not only with their spring blooms but also with their foliage, which often changes colour through the seasons. White-flowered periwinkle (*Vinca minor* 'Alba') and tiarella (in the background) associate well with it.

Opposite: A colourful planting can be achieved even in shade. Welsh poppies (*Meconopsis cambrica*) are inclined to be invasive but look fine with forget-me-nots (*Myosotis*), honesty (*Lunaria annua*) and Bowles' golden grass (*Hakonechloa macra* 'Aureola'.

PLANTS FOR POOR SOILS

Almost all soils are relatively poor, unless you happen to live in a volcanic area where mineral nutrients are plentiful, or on rich alluvial silt that has been deposited by nourishing soil particles falling out of water in a flood plain. Soil improvement is, therefore, an integral part of normal gardening management and it consists of building up the organic content, enhancing the fertility and thus making a pleasant home for the micro-organisms that are an essential ingredient of healthy soils. With constant care, even the heaviest clay loams can be given that sought-after crumbly texture which is free-draining but also moisture-retentive.

CLAY SOIL

Though difficult to handle and easily spoilt by compaction, clay soils, when in good heart, are probably among the most fertile. With adequate mulching to prevent their surfaces from cracking, and with plenty of bulky organic matter worked into their top layer, clay soils will retain moisture and sustain a wide variety of plants. But they are inclined to be cold, getting the new season off to a slow start, and, if abused, will become intractable and hostile to plants, setting so hard in summer as to be almost impossible to break up.

Roses are, almost without exception, lovers of heavy soils and will flower more constantly than in ground which threatens to dry out during a rain shortage. Big shrub roses can look especially imposing if allowed to grow to their natural size – though this may not be feasible in a very tiny garden. Other good outline plants include rhododendrons, especially if there is shade, Japanese quince (*Chaenomeles japonica*), most *Berberis* species and many dogwoods, particularly *Cornus mas*. Such witch-hazels as *Hamamelis mollis* enjoy heavyish conditions, flowering in the depths of winter but then forming a pleasing foliage background for such spring and summer shrubs as mock orange (*Philadelphus*) and the closely related deutzia.

Herbaceous plants which enjoy heavy soils are too numerous to list but outstanding examples of great ones include *Acanthus spinosus*, which associates well with the gorgeous pink Queen Anne's lace (*Chaerophyllum hirsutum* 'Roseum'). For tall spires in shades of deep, dusky blue, try the monkshoods (*Aconitum*), which are all superb, including the curious climbing species, *A. volubile*. They are also poisonous, however. Continuing the blue and pink theme, most of the cranesbills (*Geranium*) make a long-lasting, colourful understorey, but if you want to introduce a range of warmer colours, consider the day lilies (*Hemerocallis*), in oranges, russets and yellows, and site them with the glowing *Euphorbia griffithii* 'Fireglow' and, perhaps, with the South African *Phygelius aequalis*. In autumn, the toad lilies (*Tricyrtis formosana*) provide interest, making a darker contrast with late-flowering crocosmias and the stately green grass, *Helictotrichon sempervirens*. Among the host of good foliage plants, one that distinguishes itself from all others is *Lysimachia ciliata* 'Firecracker', a loosestrife with dark khaki foliage which makes a ravishing foil for the golden yellow blooms in summer.

Right: The colourful deadnettle (*Lamium maculatum*) blooms for months on heavy soil, and has been joined at summer's end by the white *Colchicum speciosum*.

CHALKY SOIL

It is much easier to make acid soil alkaline, by adding lime, than to make chalky soil acid. Mixing flowers of sulphur will result in a small and temporary fall in pH but it is better to select plants that actually enjoy lime, rather than trying to change nature. And fortunately there are many of these!

With very few exceptions, most trees will cope with alkaline soil, though many will find the dryness of free-draining chalk challenging. All members of the rose family – hawthorns, cherries, apples and pears – are quite happy on chalky soil. Maples are generally less happy, but certain species – *Acer campestre* and the larger *A. pseudoplatanus* – are fine on lime or chalk and associate well with most of the popular spring-flowering shrubs. Few shrubs, other than rhododendrons, pieris or camellias, will languish but clematis, honeysuckles (*Lonicera*), most daphnes, currants (*Ribes*), fuchsias and mahonias all enjoy chalk or lime soils.

Pinks and carnations (*Dianthus* species), the prettiest of the smaller perennials, are happier on chalk than anywhere else and make good companions for penstemons, which seem fond of chalk even though many of them hail from acid soils. They also associate well with most of the bellflowers (*Campanula*), poppies (*Papaver*) and, for the end of summer, Japanese anemones (*Anemone* x *hybrida*).

Above: In this part of the author's garden, the soil is intensely alkaline. By selecting such lime-tolerant plants as *Euphorbia characias*, lavender and red valerian (*Centranthus ruber*), a lush, colourful effect has been achieved.

111

Above: Though wind is damaging, the choice of attractive plants that cope with a regular buffeting is fairly extensive. Here, kniphofias and honesty (*Lunaria annua*) form the basis of a rugged planting.

PLANTS FOR WINDY SITES

If you have spectacular views from your windows, or you live by the sea, expect wind! But if you want to garden on a hilltop, or in the middle of a treeless plain, or at the seaside, you will have no choice but to arrange for sheltering plants. Your outline planting, therefore, needs to be functional as well as beautiful and you must select species which can shrug off the gales, or the milder but salt-laden winds, but which will not rob your soil of all its sustenance. There is no need to sacrifice a view, especially if you arrange to have strategically sited breaks in the shelter.

WINDY OR EXPOSED SITES

Many conifers are fine for shelter, but avoid Leyland cypress (*Cupressocyparis leylandii*): though it can make an excellent screen and is perfectly manageable when clipped every year, it is inclined to be weak at the root and, as it matures, will tend to crack and blow over. One of its parents, *Cupressus macrocarpa*, is an excellent hedging plant, though it is not hardy enough to survive continuous severe frosts. Beech (*Fagus*) and hornbeam (*Carpinus*) are also fine for sheltering hedges, as are Lawson's cypresses, in their various forms, and common cherry laurel (*Prunus laurocerasus*).

Within the shelter, your choice need not be limited, but, while the trees and shrubs are developing, other windproof plants which could be planted at once include cortaderia, cotoneaster, *Hypericum* 'Hidcote' and most elders. Of these, a joint planting of golden- and dark-leaved forms of elder (*Sambucus nigra* 'Aurea' and *S. nigra* 'Guincho Purple') are very effective, especially if they are pollarded by cutting them very hard back to a low stump, every second season: flowers then adorn the shrubs one year, followed, after the winter prune, by a forest of lush young vegetative growths.

One advantage of windy sites is that they are often less frost-prone than low, sheltered gardens so, if you live in a relatively mild district, you can afford to try phormiums, Mount Etna broom (*Genista aetnensis*) which grows into a graceful, pendulous tree smothered with yellow blossoms and daisy bushes (*Olearia*).

Windproof herbaceous plants will become less essential as your shelter grows but species that are especially resilient to wind, as they are to so many adverse conditions, are the dependable cranesbills. Those like *Geranium endressii*, *G. sanguineum* and *G. macrorrhizum* which occur naturally in exposed habitats, are well adapted to rough weather. Alchemillas are natural companions for these and will seed around freely, blending their pale green flowers with the pinks and mauves of the cranesbills. *Roscoea cautleyoides*, a surprisingly cooperative plant that looks far more delicate than it really is, produces in summer 25cm (10in) spikes of orchid-like flowers in rich butter yellow.

MARITIME SITES

A seaside garden can present not only the best but also the worst of conditions. Salt-laden wind can be very destructive, damaging plants by blasting them with blown sand which, in a bad storm, can be over the garden fence like a snowdrift. Against that misfortune comes the huge advantage that the sea has, with its tempering effect on the weather. In midwinter, when frost may have the whole country within its grip a kilometre or two inland, the coastal temperatures can sometimes stay above freezing throughout the period. If, like the west coast of Britain and Northern Europe, the shores are washed with a warm current – in this case, the North Atlantic Drift – the beneficial effect is doubled, enabling tender plants to be grown at surprisingly northern latitudes. Thus, in western Scotland and even Norway subtropical plants thrive in some sheltered coastal sites.

Selecting salt-tolerant species as part of the windbreak planting will go a long way to solving the problem, not only of storms but also of deposited sand. Escallonia, *Griselinia littoralis*, sea buckthorn (*Hippophae rhamnoides*) and *Fuchsia magellanica* are all examples of attractive plants which do not suffer too much from salty winds. Others, not necessarily all sheltering species but those which enjoy life by the seaside, include centranthus, erigeron, lavatera, cordyline, *Coronilla valentina* subsp. *glauca*, *Bupleurum fruticosum*, *Euonymus japonica*, *Arbutus unedo*, *Poncirus trifoliata* and most hebes. Once these plants are established and the shelter is working, the number of new species you can introduce into your manufactured microclimate is almost without limit, because a maritime garden, once it is adequately sheltered, provides the richest planting choices of all.

Left: Film maker and artist Derek Jarman created a unique garden on the windswept shingle of the English south coast. Opium poppies and seakale are perfectly at home among his *objets trouvés* and are resistant to both wind and salt spray.

A HOT, DRY GRAVEL GARDEN

Drought-prone, hungry soil can present problems, especially in a part of the garden which is inclined to dry up and bake hard in summer sun. But the same site can present a unique planting opportunity for plant species which hail from a Mediterranean climate – that is, any region where summers are hot and dry but winters cool and wet. Using sharp gravel will not only enhance the garden's appearance but also create better drainage for the plants. Mid-spring is the best time for the hundreds of species of Mediterranean bulbs which pop up rapidly through the gravel to flower as soon as the days begin to warm up. These are soon followed by dwarf bearded irises and flowering thymes. Year-round profile in this garden is provided by shrubs such as silver-leaved cotton lavender (*Santolina*), coloured sages (*Salvia*) and evergreen rock roses (*Cistus*) as well as by dramatic clumps of phormiums and yuccas.

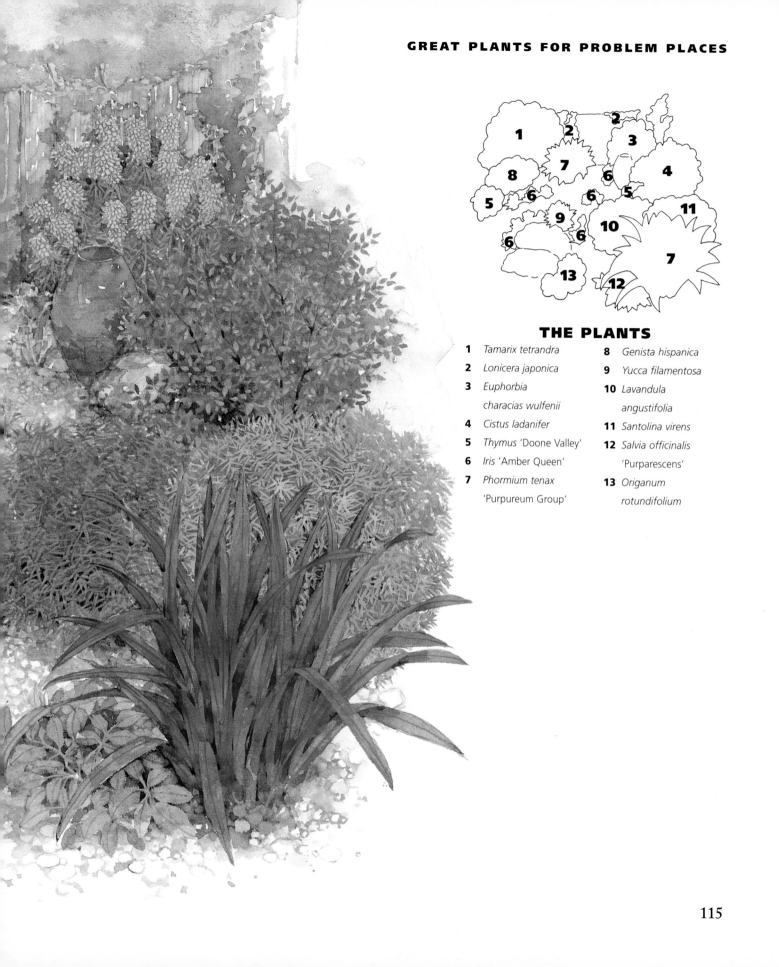

THE PLANTS

1 *Tamarix tetrandra*

2 *Lonicera japonica*

3 *Euphorbia
charjacias wulfenii*

4 *Cistus ladanifer*

5 *Thymus* 'Doone Valley'

6 *Iris* 'Amber Queen'

7 *Phormium tenax*
'Purpureum Group'

8 *Genista hispanica*

9 *Yucca filamentosa*

10 *Lavandula
angustifolia*

11 *Santolina virens*

12 *Salvia officinalis*
'Purparescens'

13 *Origanum
rotundifolium*

THE GREAT PLANT GUIDE

The key plants are the raw material with which the gardener works – like the clots of paint on an artist's palette, the raw clay in a potter's hands or the instrumental sounds and harmonics that a composer can turn into music. The ability to compose the green symphony that every good garden should be depends on a working knowledge of the plants themselves. You do not have to be a trained botanist or even an expert horticulturalist to be able to plant creatively but it is useful to know which plants are appropriate for your needs. When developing a planting in shade, for example, it helps to be familiar with at least a hardcore of woodland species that will suit your climate and conditions. If you are working in a particular colour theme, it helps to understand that the blue of a cornflower or a gentian is purer and more intense than that of most cranesbills or campanulas. Such distinctions may seem subtle but in a small space they can make a great difference to the general effect.

For gardeners the world over, the choice of plants has never been wider or more varied. In Europe alone, a minimum of 65,000 species, varieties and cultivars are documented as being commerically available, most from specialist nurseries but many also from more general suppliers such as garden centres. Of these, the plants that can be termed 'great' are numerous, but what follows is a digest of plants that are not only especially lovely for their own sakes but which are in every way outstanding for small gardens. Most plants in this final chapter have been mentioned elsewhere in the book. The purpose of The Great Plant Guide is to back up those brief appearances with a descriptive entry that provides a snapshot of each plant's vital statistics. You will find the dimensions, preferences of site, soil type and conditions listed for each plant, along with the best propagation method and any notable problems associated with it.

Above: *Papaver* 'Mrs Perry' is but one of a huge range of excellent forms of oriental poppy, providing warm colours for early summer.

Opposite: The variegated foliage of *Hosta fortunei* makes a simple but effective association with *Corydalis flexuosa*. Their leaf shapes and texture – broad and smooth against divided and fern-like – make a superb contrast, whereas the blue corydalis flowers harmonize well with the cream of the hosta foliage.

The directory is divided into the following main groups:

ALPINES Includes small perennials.

ANNUALS & BIENNIALS All non-woody plants that can only be reproduced from seed – that is, that germinate, flower, seed and die within a single season (annuals) or two seasons (biennials).

BULBS Includes plants which grow from bulbs, corms or tubers to flower at any time of year.

CLIMBERS Plants which need support through which to scramble, including woody and herbaceous climbers and creepers.

CONIFERS Coniferous shrubs and trees.

FERNS A small but choice selection.

PERENNIALS Non-woody, herbaceous plants that have a perennial rootstock, including ground-cover plants and such tender perennials as pelargoniums.

SHRUBS From low-growing dwarf species to those large enough to be pruned and used as small trees.

TREES Concentrating on specimen or outline trees.

HARDINESS CATEGORIES

1   Plants require heated glass.
2   Plants require unheated glass.
3   Plants are hardy outside in some regions or particular situations or, while usually grown outside in summer, need protection from frost in winter.
4   Plants are hardy throughout the British Isles and most of Europe.

ALPINES

AJUGA REPTANS
Ground-hugging, creeping perennial with glossy, puckered foliage, sometimes coloured or marked, forming weedproof mats. Lipped flowers are produced on 15cm (6in) spikes, deep blue or pink, from spring to autumn. This is an ideal understorey plant, making carpets in semi-shade.
HEIGHT 15–60cm (6–24in) CULTIVATION Sun or semi-shade. Prefers moist soil. PROPAGATION Division. HARDINESS 4. 'Braunherz' Bronze leaves turning reddish in autumn. 'Burgundy Glow' Leaves marked pink, cream and green.

AJUGA REPTANS 'BURGUNDY GLOW'

CAMPANULA Bellflower
(see also Perennials)
C. carpatica **Compact summer-flowering perennials with large, open bells in blue or white, held over leafy clumps.**
HEIGHT 20–30cm (8–12in). CULTIVATION Sun. Any soil but not too dry. PROPAGATION Seed or division. HARDINESS 4.
C. cochleariifolia **Mat-forming perennials with small, shiny leaves; stems carry successions of tiny blue or white bellflowers which hang, spring to summer.**

HEIGHT 10–45cm (4–18in) CULTIVATION Sun. Any soil. PROPAGATION Seed or division. HARDINESS 4.
'Elizabeth Oliver' Double-flowered form in soft blue.

DRYAS OCTOPETALA
Low, spreading perennial forming dense mats; shiny evergreen foliage, like little oak leaves with mealy white undersides. Cream rose-like blooms in early summer are followed by feathery seedheads. HEIGHT 7–60cm (3–24in). CULTIVATION Sun. Any soil. PROPAGATION Seed or cuttings. HARDINESS 4.

HACQUETIA EPIPACTIS
Compact perennial with distinctive rounded foliage among which come golden-green flowers at winter's end, each nestling in a ruff of green foliage. Seeds freely in moist shade. Charming with spring bulbs.
HEIGHT 15–30cm (6–12in). CULTIVATION Shade or partial shade. Leafy soil, not too dry. PROPAGATION Seed or division. HARDINESS 4.

HELIANTHEMUM Garden hybrids
Low, sprawling sub-shrubs with small, narrow silvery or dark green leaves on tough wiry stems, which set off flowers that last only a day. Cut back after flowering to keep plants compact and ensure a flush of foliage for autumn. Of value from spring to summer; good in silver foliage schemes.
HEIGHT 20–60cm (8–24in). CULTIVATION Sun. Any dry soil. PROPAGATION Cuttings. HARDINESS 4.
'Mrs C.W. Earle' Scarlet-red, double-flowered form. 'Raspberry Ripple' Pink flowers with white markings against soft, grey foliage. 'Wisley Primrose' Large, pale yellow flowers, almost 3cm (1¼in) across.

ORIGANUM 'KENT BEAUTY'

HEPATICA TRANSSILVANICA

Compact perennial with anemone-like, sky-blue flowers, 2cm (1in) across, produced on short stems in early spring, followed by rounded, lobed leaves. Trim off previous season's leaves in late winter to maximize floral display. A star performer for shade. HEIGHT 15–30cm (6–12in). CULTIVATION Partial shade. Moist, leafy soil. PROPAGATION Seed or division of the tuberous roots. HARDINESS 4.

IRIS PUMILA

Dwarf bearded iris which flowers in late spring. Divide regularly to keep flowering. HEIGHT Up to 25cm (10in). CULTIVATION Sun. Any free-draining soil. PROPAGATION Division. HARDINESS 4.
'Austrian Skies' Flowers pale blue. 'Blue Denim' Petals blue, russet beard. 'Little Bill' Beige to brown falls, lilac-blue beard.

LITHODORA OLEIFOLIA

Compact sub-shrub with silvery green foliage, darkening with age; in summer clusters of small, cup-shaped pale blue flowers, slightly pink in the bud, held gracefully above the foliage. HEIGHT 15–20cm (6–8in). CULTIVATION Sun. Any free-draining soil. PROPAGATION Seed or cuttings. HARDINESS 4.

OMPHALODES

O. cappadocica Compact perennial with grey to dark green, silver-backed foliage and, in spring, ample displays of vivid blue flowers, shaped like forget-me-nots, but up to 2cm (1in) across.
HEIGHT 15–20cm (6–8in). CULTIVATION Sun or partial shade. Fertile free-draining soil. PROPAGATION Seed. HARDINESS 4.
O. verna As above but with spreading rootstock, broader, greener leaves, slightly smaller flowers. There is a white form too.

ORIGANUM

O. laevigatum Perennial with dark green foliage and purple to black stems which produce large, loose sprays of tiny purple-pink blooms for much of the summer. HEIGHT 30–45cm (12–18in). CULTIVATION Sun. Free-draining soil. PROPAGATION Seed, cuttings or division. HARDINESS 4.
O. rotundifolium Low, twiggy perennial with neat, rounded leaves on prostrate stems which end in intriguing apple-green bracts, resembling fresh hops, concealing tiny mauve to pink flowers (summer). Will succumb to a severe winter. HEIGHT: 12–25cm (5–10in.) CULTIVATION Sun. Free-draining soil. PROPAGATION Seed or cuttings. HARDINESS 3.

PRIMULA (*see also Perennials*)

P. auricula Perennial with fragrant five-petalled spring flowers in muted colours including beige, maroon, purple, rusty red and yellow. Selected seedlings often make better garden subjects than named show varieties. Take offshoots regularly to ensure young plants. HEIGHT Up to 15–20cm (6–8in). CULTIVATION Sun or part shade. Free-draining soil. PROPAGATION Seed or division. HARDINESS 4.
P. vernalis (primroses and polyanthus)

Almost every one of these perennials is desirable for the small garden in spring, including cowslips *(P. veris)*, oxslips *(P. elatior)* and primroses *(P. vulgaris)*. *Primula* 'Wanda' (magenta primrose) and *P.* 'Guinevere' (lilac polyanthus with dark foliage) are but two of a host of superb old-fashioned primulas. All need to be divided each year, after flowering, and replanted. HEIGHT 15–20cm (6–8in). CULTIVATION Sun or part shade. Rich, leafy soil, not too hot in summer. PROPAGATION Seed or division. HARDINESS 4.

PULSATILLA VULGARIS Pasque flower

Perennial with feathery foliage and nodding spring flowers, slightly hairy on reverse of petals, in lilac-mauve to purple (maroon red in the variety 'Rubra') with bold golden stamens; followed by feathery seedheads in early summer. HEIGHT 20cm (8in). CULTIVATION Sun. Free-draining soil. PROPAGATION Seed. HARDINESS 4.

RANUNCULUS FICARIA

Lesser celandine
Regarded as a weed by some, this plant has interesting garden forms including 'Brazen Hussy', with dark purple-black leaves, and 'Cupreus', with orange flowers. Flowers in spring; petals have a high sheen. HEIGHT 10–20cm (4–8in). CULTIVATION Sun or shade. Moist soil. PROPAGATION Division. HARDINESS 4.

SEDUM (*see also Perennials*)

S. kamtschaticum Valuable drought-resistant creeping perennials with fleshy foliage, semi-prostrate stems and flat-topped, yellow blooms; year-round interest. HEIGHT: 7.5cm (3in). CULTIVATION Sun. Dry, poor soil. PROPAGATION Division or cuttings. HARDINESS 4.

ANNUALS & BIENNIALS

CALENDULA Pot marigold
Pungently aromatic foliage and bright, rayed flowers in warm orange or yellow tones; prolific self-seeders. Good series include: 'Art Shades', 'Touch of Red', 'Radio'.
HEIGHT 30–45cm (12–18in). CULTIVATION
Sun. Free-draining soil. PROPAGATION
Seed. HARDINESS 4.

CENTAUREA CYANUS Cornflower
Silvery foliage and erect, but weak, stems topped with distinctive blue florets in a whorl above the flask-shaped seed capsule, in summer. Other colours include pink, white and dark purple; dwarf series too.
HEIGHT 45–60cm (18–24in). CULTIVATION
Sun. Free-draining, fertile soil.
PROPAGATION Seed. HARDINESS 4.

COSMOS
Filigree green foliage and showy, yellow-centred flowers with bold outer rays in pink, white or maroon, in summer. Start off in trays and plant out in late spring.
HEIGHT 60–90cm (2–3ft). CULTIVATION
Sun. Free-draining fertile soil.
PROPAGATION Seed. HARDINESS 4.

DIGITALIS Foxglove
D. purpurea **From large, rough-looking foliage, velvety to the touch, emerge tall spires of tubular summer flowers, many with speckled throats and purple-flushed outsides. White and pale pink forms even more desirable than the wild purple kind.**
HEIGHT 45–60cm (2–3ft). CULTIVATION
Shade or part-shade. Any soil.
PROPAGATION Seed (biennial). HARDINESS 4.
'Sutton's Apricot' Unique apricot blooms.
D. x mertonensis Hybrid with blooms the colour of crushed strawberry. *D. ferruginea* Distinctive species with rusty, lipped flowers.

ESCHSCHOLZIA Californian poppy
Vivid blooms among greyish lacy foliage in summer. Great self-seeder; autumn and spring sowing ensures long-lasting display. Try 'Mission Bells' and 'Apricot Flambeau'.
HEIGHT 30–45cm (12–18in). CULTIVATION
Sun Any free-draining soil. PROPAGATION
Seed. HARDINESS 4.

ESCHSCHOLZIA 'MISSION BELLS'

LIMNANTHES DOUGLASII
Carpets of emerald-green ferny foliage are blotted out, in late spring, by vivid yellow-centred white flowers. Self-seeds wildly.
 HEIGHT 10–15cm (4–6in). CULTIVATION
Sun or part-shade. Free-draining, fertile soil.
PROPAGATION Seed. HARDINESS 4.

LUNARIA ANNUA Honesty
Cross-shaped, purple blooms emerge on branched stems from broad basal leaves in spring. In autumn, the flattened, transparent seed capsules make a second display. Useful for carpeting the understorey, below shrubs.
HEIGHT 45–60cm (18–24in). CULTIVATION
Sun or part-shade. Any soil but not too dry.
PROPAGATION Seed. HARDINESS 4.
'Alba Variegata' Pale-cream-dashed foliage and white flowers make this form perfect for brightening a dull corner.

NICOTIANA Tobacco plant
Perennials, best grown as annuals, with soft, sometimes glutinous, foliage and in summer trumpet flowers which are often fragrant, especially at night.
HEIGHT Various: 30–60cm (12–24in).
CULTIVATION Sun. Any soil. PROPAGATION
Seed. HARDINESS 2 or 3.
N. sylvestris Very tall species (120cm/4ft or more) with huge leaves and hanging sprays of white blooms which persist all summer. Prolific seeder but not hardy. *N. langsdorffii* Green flowers with eye-catching blue stamens; 60cm (2ft) high.
'Domino' series Low growing (30cm/12in) compact varieties whose colours include near red and salmon pink.

PAPAVER Poppy
P. rhoeas **Great varieties include the 'Shirley' series, whose summer flowers have ruffled petals in soft pinks or picotees with lemon pollen; 'Mother of Pearl' series has flowers in various dusky tones from dull maroon to a light pinkish-grey; 'Angel Choir' is similar but with double flowers. Best when allowed to seed freely, creating natural drifts in a mixed border.**
HEIGHT 45cm (18in) or more. CULTIVATION
Sun. Any soil. PROPAGATION Seed.
HARDINESS 4.
P. somniferum Glaucous foliage and bright flowers in red, pink, white or magenta.

TROPAEOLUM MAJUS Nasturtium
Rounded leaves which smell like capers and vivid flowers in reddish-orange or yellow, produced along scrambling stems throughout summer. Vigorous and spreading.
HEIGHT 20cm (8in), spreading.
CULTIVATION Sun. Any soil, not too rich.
PROPAGATION Seed. HARDINESS 4.
'Alaska' Variegated foliage, compact habit.

BULBS

AGAPANTHUS

Summer-flowering bulbs with a tall, single stem and flowers in blue, or sometimes white, umbels. Raised from several South African species including *A. inapertus* **(whose flowers hang downwards) and the larger-flowered** *A. africanus.*
HEIGHT Various, 30–90cm (1–3ft).
CULTIVATION Sun. Warm soil. PROPAGATION Division or seed. HARDINESS 3.
A. 'Headbourne Hybrids' are lower growing, with smaller flowerheads, and hardier than the larger species, but all agapanthus need protection from extremes of frost.

ALLIUM

A large, valuable tribe with drumstick-shaped flowers on erect stems in spring and summer. Colours range through pinks and purples; also yellow species. On many, the leaves start to die back before flowers appear, so plant bulbs where their bases will be concealed by other plants.
HEIGHT Various 7–90cm (3in–3ft).
CULTIVATION Sun. Free-draining soil.
PROPAGATION Seed. HARDINESS 3 or 4.
A. aflatunense Deep purple flowers on tall stems in late spring. *A. christophii* Huge, silvery-lilac drumsticks in late spring. *A. karataviense* Richly coloured, broad foliage

ANEMONE BLANDA 'WHITE SPLENDOUR'

precedes off-white blooms. *A. siculum* (now *Nectaroscordium siculum*) Pink and green flowers hang elegantly atop 1m (3ft) stems.

ANEMONE (*see also Perennials*)

Modest growth, ferny foliage and gem-like spring blooms make these plants perfect for small gardens.
HEIGHT 10–25cm (4–10in). CULTIVATION Sun or part-shade. Any soil. PROPAGATION Seed or tubers. HARDINESS 4.
A. blanda Daisy-like flowers in early spring, often blue but 'White Splendour' is one of the best; prefer shade. *A. coronaria* Florist anemones, including 'De Caen' (single flowers) and 'Saint Brigid' (doubles) which can be red, blue, mauve or white. *A. fulgens* Startling scarlet blooms in mid-spring.
A. nemorosa Shade-loving species with creeping roots and white flowers; 'Allenii' has gorgeous lilac blooms.

CHIONODOXA Glory-of-the-snow

Low-growing species with several 2cm/1in sky-blue, white-centred blooms on each short stem in spring. Best planted in drifts and allowed to naturalize. All species are good, especially *C. luciliae* **(pale blue) and** *C. sardensis* **(darker blue).**
HEIGHT 10cm (4in) or more. CULTIVATION Sun. Free-draining soil. PROPAGATION Bulbs or seed. HARDINESS 4.

COLCHICUM

Crocus-like blooms in mauve or white appear without foliage in autumn. Large, dark green leaves emerge in spring and can be used as foliage plants. Best garden forms: *C. speciosum* **and** *C. s.* **'Album'. There is also a double, 'Waterlily'.**
HEIGHT Foliage 30-45cm (12–18in); flowers up to 15cm (6in). CULTIVATION Sun or part-shade. Any soil. PROPAGATION Bulbs.
HARDINESS 4.

COLCHICUM SPECIOSUM

CROCUS

Valuable for colour in late winter and spring, their exquisite chalice-shaped flowers open wide, often revealing different colours, to greet the sun. Most effective when naturalized in grass.
HEIGHT Up to 10–20cm (4–8in).
CULTIVATION Sun. Any soil. PROPAGATION Seed or corms. HARDINESS 4.
C. chrysanthus Various shades including yellow, cream and blue, in late winter.
C. speciosus Violet-blue with prominent orange stigmas, autumn-flowering.
C. tommasinianus 'Whitewell Purple' Winter blooming. *C. vernus* Large Dutch kinds include 'Jeanne d'Arc', white, and 'Pickwick', purple striped.

CYCLAMEN

C. coum **Compact, with rounded foliage, often marked with silver, and small pink, carmine or white blooms in midwinter.**
HEIGHT 10–15cm (4–6in). CULTIVATION Sun or shade. Any free-draining soil.
PROPAGATION Seed. HARDINESS 4.
C. hederifolium **Handsome ivy-shaped leaves, marbled with grey and silver, from winter to late spring. Pink or white flowers, with swept-back petals, appear in autumn; some forms are fragrant. Gem-like flowers make a winter splash.**
HEIGHT 15–25cm (6–10in). CULTIVATION Sun or shade. Any soil. PROPAGATION Seed.
HARDINESS 4.

FRITILLARIA

F. imperialis Crown imperial. **Rapid-growing, thick stems carry, at their tops, bunches of orange or yellow bell-shaped spring flowers up to 5cm (2in) across, beneath a topknot of foliage. Architectural shape to accompany spring bulbs.** HEIGHT 60–90cm (2–3ft). CULTIVATION Sun. Any soil. PROPAGATION Bulbs. HARDINESS 4.

F. meleagris Snakeshead fritillary. **Narrow foliage; thin stems carry nodding brown-purple, bell-shaped blooms marked with tiny white chequers in spring. Many forms, running through pale dusky mauve to greenish-white. Naturalizes well in grass.** HEIGHT 10–25cm (4–10in). CULTIVATION Sun. Any soil. PROPAGATION Seed or bulbs. HARDINESS 4.

GALANTHUS Snowdrop

Charming small winter-flowering bulbs with nodding white flowers. HEIGHT 15–20cm (6–8in). CULTIVATION Shade or partial shade. Any soil. PROPAGATION Bulbs or seed. HARDINESS 4.

G. elwesii Earlier blooming, larger in flower and leaf, with more conspicuous green markings on the flowers; to 25cm (10in) tall. *G. nivalis* Pure white, honey-scented flowers, tipped with green markings, blooming mid- to late winter. 'S. Arnott' A huge, scented snowdrop. 'Ophelia'

IRIS 'KATHARINE HODGKIN'

A dramatic, double cultivar, whose flower centres make tightly packed green rosettes.

GALTONIA CANDICANS

Imposing white flowers hang along the tops of sturdy, erect stems in midsummer. HEIGHT 20–60cm (8–24in). CULTIVATION Sun. Warm, well-drained soil. PROPAGATION Seed. HARDINESS 4.

GLADIOLUS

Sword-like foliage and flowers with petals in threes, arranged tightly against the stems, in late summer and autumn. Species often more handsome than exhibition hybrids which look coarse in small gardens. HEIGHT 30–60cm (1–2ft). CULTIVATION Sun. Free-draining soil. PROPAGATION Corms. HARDINESS 4.

G. callianthus 'Mureliae' Fragrant white late-flowering blooms with deep purple-blue centres hanging on extended stems.

IPHEION UNIFLORUM

Low, curled strap-shaped leaves with garlic aroma and a mass of faded blue to white flowers throughout spring. Forms include 'Wisley Blue' and 'Froyle Mill' (violet). HEIGHT 10cm (4in), spreading. CULTIVATION Sun. Dry, free-draining soil. PROPAGATION Bulbs or seed. HARDINESS 4.

IRIS *(See also Alpines and Perennials)*

Reticulata group **Tribe of tiny winter-flowering irises with flowers in distinctive three-part shapes in strong colours, often marked with speckles or splashes of contrasting colour. Look for *I. reticulata*, dark blue with yellow markings; 'J.S. Dijt', magenta; 'Katharine Hodgkin', greenish-blue with leopard markings.** HEIGHT 10–15cm (4–6in). CULTIVATION Sun. Any soil. PROPAGATION Bulbs. HARDINESS 4.

LILIUM MARTAGON

LILIUM

A huge genus with hundreds of great plants; excellent for containers. HEIGHT 30–90cm (1–3ft). CULTIVATION Sun or partial shade. Rich, fertile soil; some species dislike lime. PROPAGATION Seed, bulbils or scales. HARDINESS 4.

L. candidum Madonna lily. Foliage emerges in autumn, flower spikes in midsummer, carrying clusters of pure white, fragrant blooms. *L. henryi* Lime-tolerant. Apricot blooms, with reflexed petals, in summer on 2m (6ft) stems. *L. lancifolium* Tiger lily. Lime-tolerant. Orange, richly spotted blooms. 1.5m (5ft). *L. martagon* Turkscap lily. Pink or cream spotted petals in early summer. Prefers partial shade.

MUSCARI Grape hyacinth

Useful genus whose mainly blue, rounded flowers cluster along the stems in spring, resembling tiny bunches of azure grapes. HEIGHT 7.5–20cm (3–8in). CULTIVATION Sun or shade. Any soil. PROPAGATION Bulbs or seed. HARDINESS 4.

M. botryoides 'Alba' A neat-growing white form, ideal for pale planting schemes.

NARCISSUS Daffodil

Among the most popular and valuable of all bulbs, their cheerful colours are the making of spring. In a small garden, the aftermath of their foliage can be unsightly unless the bulbs are carefully placed. There are desirable narcissi for small spaces in all the different groups, as follows:

TRUMPET NARCISSUS Large in bloom with an untidy aftermath of leaves. 'King Alfred' and 'Unsurpassable', both golden yellow; 'Mount Hood', white; 'Spellbinder', lemon: a reverse bicolor, trumpet paler than perianth.

LARGE-CUPPED NARCISSUS Large varieties, many with contrasting cup and perianth colours. 'Passionale', white with pink cup; 'Carlton', orange and yellow bicolor; 'Professor Einstein', white, red cup.

SMALL-CUPPED NARCISSUS 'Verger' has red cups against a stark white background. 'Rockall' has softer orange centre, off-white background; 'Cheerfulness', double flowers.

TRIANDRUS NARCISSUS White or pale yellow hanging blooms with dainty, flared cups. 'Thalia', a tall white form; 'Hawera', lemon yellow, 20cm (8in) stems; good with muscari.

NARCISSUS CYCLAMINEUS GROUP Swept-back petals and compact habit make them ideal for small gardens. 'February Gold' and 'Peeping Tom', early, golden-yellow; 'February Silver' and 'Dove Wings', cream fading white.

JONQUILS Late-flowering, richly fragrant, small flattened blooms with rounded petals and tiny cups. Foliage narrow, neat and often deep green. 'Bobbysoxer', a dependable late bloomer with pale yellow flowers and strong fragrance. The pure species *N. jonquilla* and *N. uncifolius* are also desirable.

NARCISSUS TAZETTA GROUP Multi-headed, fragrant species with small flowers and tiny but deep cups. 'Geranium', clusters of white blooms with orange-red cups. *Narcissus canaliculatus* is a similar species to *N. tazetta*, with softer colours – pale yellow and white.

NARCISSUS POETICUS GROUP Pure white, nicely rounded flowers, usually with a small but conspicuous red and yellow cup; many are fragrant. 'Actaea', a large, early to mid-season bloomer. Late-blooming *N. poeticus* 'Recurvus' is the true 'pheasant's eye', with a heavy fragrance and elegantly reflexed petals.

WILD SPECIES For alpine containers, try the tiny *N. asturiensis*. Wordsworth's wild daffodils were *N. pseudonarcissus*, lower, smaller versions of the more commonly grown large trumpet plants.

TULIPA 'PRINSES IRENE'

TULIPA Tulip

Many wild species and several hybrid tulips from the different groups are perfect for small gardens in spring.

SPECIES TULIPS These are close to the flowers you might find growing wild in Turkey or South Eastern Europe. *T. pulchella* is very early, with coral-pink or purplish blooms on 10cm (4in) stems; *T. turkestanica*, early, carries several cream flowers per stem; *T. clusiana*, the lady tulip, has carmine petals, each with a silvery white edge, and opens to reveal a dark centre.

BOTANICAL TULIPS These are simple crosses or hybrids of species. **Kaufmanniana tulips**, raised from *T. kaufmanniana*, include 'Fritz Kreisler', pink and sulphur yellow; 'Stresa', vivid yellow, red and orange. **Greigii tulips** often have mottled or striped leaves and include the scarlet 'Red Riding Hood' and 'Yellow Dawn', a peach and yellow combination. **Fosteriana tulips** are among the tallest and showiest of the early flowerers: 'Madame Lefeber' has imposing scarlet blooms; 'Purissima', whose flowers are ivory, fading to white, is possibly the finest garden tulip in cultivation.

SINGLE AND DOUBLE EARLY TULIPS These have classic tulip shapes and are among the first of the hybrids to bloom. 'Prinses Irene' is great for small gardens, with its dark glaucous foliage and tan flowers; 'Bellona' is the best single early yellow; among doubles, 'Electra' is a startling pink and 'Scarlet Cardinal' the finest of the reds.

NEW DARWIN HYBRID TULIPS Best known of the classic tulips, growing tall, with generous-sized, goblet-shaped flowers. 'Apeldoorn', red, and 'Golden Apeldoorn' are both recommended.

LATE OR COTTAGE TULIPS The last group to bloom, including pure white 'Alabaster', dark purple 'Greuze' and red and white 'Union Jack'.

PARROT TULIPS The petals of this group have been affected by a benign virus to develop the feather-like qualities that have made them fashionable. 'Black Parrot', a bewitching deep violet, perfect for cutting; 'Texas Flame', red and yellow; 'Fantasy', rose, green and salmon.

LILY-FLOWERED AND VIRIDIFLORA TULIPS Lily-flowered kinds, such as 'West Point', yellow, and 'Queen of Sheba', red, edged with yellow, have pointed petals. **Viridiflora tulips** have green markings on the outsides of their petals and include 'Greenland', where the green suffuses a background of plummy pink, and 'Spring Green', which is predominantly white.

CLIMBERS

CLEMATIS

The most popular and useful genus of climbers and scramblers. Their pruning taxes some people, but such good-natured plants will rarely take exception to wrongful pruning anyway. The general rule is: if it flowers after the longest day, prune hard at winter's end. If it flowers before the longest day, pruning is not needed but, if you do prune, do so as soon as the main flowering period has finished.

CLEMATIS ALPINA GROUP Spring-flowering species with nodding blooms which are half-open: 'Frances Rivis', large blue flowers, with cream centres; 'Columbine', pale blue; 'Burford White'; 'Helsingborg', royal blue.

CLEMATIS CIRRHOSA Winter-flowering with small, pale blooms on semi-evergreen plants. Not fully hardy. 'Freckles' A form with rusty blotches in the flower.

LARGE-FLOWERED HYBRIDS Early flowering: 'Countess of Lovelace', soft lavender-blue blooms, the first flush of which are double, the later flowers single; 'H.F. Young', pale blue, heavy crop in spring but reluctant to re-flower; 'Marie Boisselot', pure white, very large flowers.

LARGE- AND MEDIUM-FLOWERED HYBRIDS Later flowering: 'Huldine', white, medium flowers with a touch of blue in some lights; x *jackmanii* 'Superba', deep purple-blue flowers, great vigour; x *durandii*, satin-like, deep blue flowers.

CLEMATIS VITICELLA HYBRIDS The most useful for growing through other host plants since they are cut back hard every autumn or spring. 'Madame Julia Correvon', ruby red, mid-sized flowers; 'Alba Luxurians', flowers white, edged with green; 'Minuet', small flowers, purplish-red with paler pink to white centres; 'Betty Corning', softest lavender-mauve with a touch of ash grey.

CLEMATIS CIRRHOSA 'FRECKLES'

CLEMATIS MONTANA Invasive, but can be controlled by pruning back immediately after flowering. 'Elizabeth', pale pink; 'Marjorie', salmon-flecked greenish-white, semi-double; *C.m. sericea*, the finest white sub-species (formerly known as *C. spooneri*); 'Tetrarose', deep pink.

ORANGE PEEL CLEMATIS 'Bill Mackenzie', mustard-yellow blooms followed by fluffy seedheads; *C. tangutica*, bright yellow flowers, shaped like Chinese lanterns.

CLEMATIS TEXENSIS Herbaceous species which need cutting back to ground level each year. 'Etoile Rose', delicate pink to cherry-red blooms shaped like small tulips; 'Gravetye Beauty', tulip-shaped blooms in glowing wine red; 'Duchess of Albany', vigorous, with pale pink blooms.

COBAEA SCANDENS

Vigorous climber with large, bell-shaped flowers in greenish-white or purple-blue and shapely seedheads in autumn.
HEIGHT To 4m (12ft). CULTIVATION Sun or shade. Any soil. PROPAGATION Seed. HARDINESS 3.

ECCREMOCARPUS SCABER

Moderately vigorous with pretty, ferny foliage and a succession of clusters of brilliantly coloured tubular flowers throughout summer. Colours include yellow, orange, salmon and wine red.
HEIGHT To 3m (9ft). CULTIVATION Sun. Any fertile soil. PROPAGATION Seed. HARDINESS 3.

HEDERA Ivy

Hardy, vigorous evergreen creepers which cling by adventitious roots. Invaluable for their tolerance of deep, dry shade.
HEIGHT To 4m (12ft). CULTIVATION Shade. Any soil. PROPAGATION Layers or cuttings. HARDINESS 4.

H. colchica Portuguese ivy. Large leaves, up to 25cm (10in) across. 'Sulphur Heart' Suffusions of lime green through the foliage. *H. helix* English ivy. Three-pointed foliage when in the climbing stage, becoming woody later as flower shoots emerge. Many finely decorative forms: 'Adam' and 'Heise', both white- and green-variegated; 'Ivalace', ruffled green leaves; 'Goldchild', yellow variegations.

HUMULUS LUPULUS 'AUREUS'

Golden hop
Vigorous gold-leaved form of the annual hop used to make beer. Ravishing blended with dark-flowered clematis or deep red roses but often too vigorous on rich soils.
HEIGHT To 3m (9ft). CULTIVATION Sun or shade. Any soil. PROPAGATION Division. HARDINESS 4.

JASMINUM Jasmine

Moderately vigorous climbers with species for summer and winter interest.
HEIGHT To 3m (9ft). CULTIVATION Sun or shade. Any soil. PROPAGATION Layering. HARDINESS 3–4.

J. nudiflorum Winter jasmine. Yellow flowers borne on dark green stems through the darkest months; stems root where they touch the ground.

J. officinale Summer jastmine. Constant run of fragrant white blooms from midsummer onwards. Best grown alone. Hardiness 3, so needs winter protection in cold areas.

LAPAGERIA ROSEA

Non-vigorous evergreen climber with long, elegant waxy red flowers in late summer. Needs a sheltered spot.
HEIGHT To 2m (6ft). CULTIVATION Shade. Leafy, acid soil. PROPAGATION Cuttings or layering. HARDINESS 3.

LONICERA Honeysuckle, woodbine

Vigorous, often fragrant climbers for spring and summer interest. Most are best if allowed to scramble freely.
HEIGHT To 4m (12ft) or less. CULTIVATION Partial or deep shade, but tolerant of sun if the roots are cool. Any soil. PROPAGATION Seed, layers or cuttings. HARDINESS 4.
L. x *brownii* Scarlet or orange tubular flowers in clusters all summer. 'Dropmore Scarlet' is dependable.
L. japonica 'Halliana' Intensely fragrant, semi-evergreen, blooming from midsummer to late autumn.
L. periclymenum Spring- and summer-flowering, with clusters of fragrant blooms, often repeated through to autumn. 'Belgica' An early variety. 'Graham Thomas' Flowers are primrose and parchment.

LONICERA PERICLYMENUM 'BELGICA'

PLUMBAGO AURICULATA

Moderately vigorous, tender African native with pale sky-blue flowers produced constantly through the summer.
HEIGHT To 2m (6ft), more in tropical climates. CULTIVATION Sun. Any soil. PROPAGATION Cuttings. HARDINESS 2.

RHODOCHITON ATROSANGUINEUS

Non-vigorous climber with garlands of strange black and purple-pink blooms in summer. A perennial but easier raised from seed each year. It needs a host plant through which to grow.
HEIGHT To 2m (6ft). CULTIVATION Sun or shade. Any soil. PROPAGATION Seed. HARDINESS 2.

SCHIZOPHRAGMA INTEGRIFOLIUM

Non-vigorous relative of hydrangea with large leaves, greyish stems and cream lacecap flowers in summer made conspicuous by large oval sterile florets. Slow to establish, but a great contributor.
HEIGHT To 1.5m (5ft). CULTIVATION Sun or shade. Moist soil. PROPAGATION Layers or cuttings. HARDINESS 4.

SOLANUM Potato vine

Non-vigorous climbers with long-lasting flowers from early to late summer.
HEIGHT To 2m (6ft). CULTIVATION Sun. Rich soil. PROPAGATION Cuttings. HARDINESS 3–4.
S. crispum Hardiest of the group: mauve to blue flowers, each with a yellow centre. 'Glasnevin' is the hardiest clone.
S. jasminoides 'Album' White-flowered climber for a sunny spot.

TROPAEOLUM

Non vigorous summer-flowering annual climber. Can be allowed to weave through evergreens such as yew or holly.

SOLANUM CRISPUM 'GLASNEVIN'

HEIGHT To 1.5m (5ft). CULTIVATION Shade. Any soil. PROPAGATION Seed. HARDINESS 3.
T. speciosum Garlands of vivid red flowers, followed by blue-black fruits. Enjoys having cool feet with its head in the sun.
T. tuberosum 'Ken Aslet' Flowers are orange and red.

VITIS VINIFERA 'PURPUREA'

Vigorous grape vine with purple foliage, greyish when very young, turning beetroot red before falling in autumn. Makes a gorgeous companion to red roses or pale clematis.
HEIGHT to 4m (12ft). CULTIVATION Sun. Any soil. PROPAGATION Cuttings or layers. HARDINESS 3.

WISTERIA

W. floribunda **Vigorous climber with exquisite lilac racemes in spring. Best grown on its own.**
HEIGHT To 7m (20ft) or more. CULTIVATION Sun. Any soil. PROPAGATION Graft only. HARDINESS 3.
'Macrobotrys' Extra long lilac racemes.
'Rosea' Pink-flowered form.
W. sinensis Chinese wisteria. As above but earlier to flower, and with shorter, plumper racemes.

CONIFERS

Though shade-tolerant, these conifers are all happiest in full light where they will retain their green branches right down to ground level for many years. Unless stated otherwise, each plant listed is fully hardy (Hardiness 4), happy in any soil and reproduced by grafts or by cuttings. All are grown for their foliage interest or their shape. Heights given are the ultimate height in a mature plant.

CHAMAECYPARIS

C. lawsoniana 'Aurea Densa' **Dwarf dome-shaped conifer, growing dense as it ages, with golden foliage.**
HEIGHT To 1.2m (3^1/$_2$ft). 'Pembury Blue': to 7m (23ft), the bluest Lawson's cypress.
C. pisifera 'Boulevard' **Semi-dwarf with blue-grey foliage, soft cylindrical twig tips and a pleasing, pyramid shape.**
HEIGHT To 3m (10ft) CULTIVATION Must have moist soil, preferably cool in summer.

CUPRESSUS MACROCARPA

Monterey cypress
Large tree, superb for hedging, but not hardy in sustained severe frost.
HEIGHT To 20m (70ft). 'Goldcrest': a lime-green form.

JUNIPERUS Juniper

J. communis 'Hibernica' (Irish juniper)
Dark green, very erect with dense branches covered in small, prickly needles.
HEIGHT To 4.5m (13^1/$_2$ft).
J. horizontalis 'Bar Harbor' **Spreading, ground-hugging dwarf juniper which will provide a constant green carpet.**
J. scopulorum 'Blue Heaven' **Medium tree with blue foliage and neat growing habit. Its ultimate shape is pyramidal.**
HEIGHT To 5m (17ft).

METASEQUOIA

GLYPTOSTROBOIDES Dawn redwood
Deciduous columnar tree, ultimately large but slow-growing; attractive when young. In dry conditions, growth is even slower.

PICEA Spruce

P. abies 'Nidiformis' **Low, flat-topped dwarf conifer with mat-forming habit.**
HEIGHT To 2m (6^1/$_2$ft) after many decades.
CULTIVATION Dislikes soil too dry.
P. glauca 'Albertiana Conica' **Short green needles; grows into a neat, conical shape so dense it looks as if it has been clipped.**
HEIGHT Dwarf to 3m (10ft).
P. pungens 'Moerheimii' **Compact, stately blue spruce. In winter the needles are an almost iridescent blue.**

PINUS Pine

P. mugo 'Gnom' Dwarf pine to 1.5 m (5ft).
P. sylvestris Scots pine. Large tree but attractive while young. HEIGHT 20m (70ft).

TAXUS BACCATA Yew

Large, spreading tree which make an excellent hedging plant.
'Fastigiata' Irish yew. Erect, narrowly columnar outline, ideal for small gardens.
'Fastigiata Aureomarginata' Golden form.

ASPLENIUM SCOLOPENDRIUM

FERNS

All ferns are grown for their foliage, which brings interest in spring and summer. They enjoy moist conditions, shade or semi-shade and leafy soil unless otherwise stated. All are reproduced most easily by division. They are all Hardiness 4 unless otherwise stated.

ADIANTUM PEDATUM

Delicate, branching maidenhair fronds.
HEIGHT 30–45cm (12–18in). CULTIVATION Though hardy, intolerant of cold winds.

ASPLENIUM

A. scolopendrium Hart's tongue fern
Solid-looking strap-shaped fronds developing in shapely rosettes.
HEIGHT 30cm (12in). CULTIVATION Tolerates a level of dryness, but dislikes sun.
A. trichomanes Maidenhair spleenwort
Happiest growing in a cool wall, where the root system can explore the crevices and produce series of tiny maidenhair fronds.
HEIGHT 10–15cm (4–6in).

ATHYRIUM FILIX-FEMINA Lady fern
The classic fern shape with 'fiddle head' buds which open into graceful fronds, bright green at first, gradually darkening.
HEIGHT 60cm (2ft).

DRYOPTERIS FILIX-MAS Male fern
Like a larger, stronger version of the lady fern with handsome fronds which develop a rusty, scaly hairiness along their length.
HEIGHT 90cm (3ft). CULTIVATION Fairly drought-tolerant, as long as it is in shade.

MATTEUCCIA STRUTHIOPTERIS

Ostrich-plume fern
Moisture-lover whose huge shuttlecock-shaped rosettes appear in spring.
HEIGHT 60–90cm (2–3ft).

PERENNIALS

ACANTHUS SPINOSUS
Handsome lobed foliage familiar from column decorations in classical design make a strong outline for summer. Tall spikes produced throughout the season bear flowers in pale lilac and green.
HEIGHT 45–120cm (18in–4ft). CULTIVATION Sun or part-shade. Rich soil. PROPAGATION Seed or division. HARDINESS 4.

ACANTHUS SPINOSUS

ACONITUM Monkshood
Tall spires of blue flowers bring interest in summer or autumn. Try with *Cimicifuga* to add colour to the late-summer understorey.
HEIGHT 45–120cm (18in–4ft). CULTIVATION Sun or part-shade. Rich soil. PROPAGATION Seed or division. HARDINESS 4.
A. carmichaelii Autumn-blooming on tall spires with blue, domed flowers shaped like the cowl on a monk's habit.
A. napellus Summer-flowering, in shades of pale or dark blue, bi-coloured blue and white (*A.* x *bicolor*) or lilac-pink ('Carneum').

ACTAEA RUBRA Baneberry
Ferny foliage and grubby white flowers precede vivid red berries.
HEIGHT 45cm (18in). CULTIVATION Shade. Any soil. PROPAGATION Seed or division. HARDINESS 4.

ALCHEMILLA MOLLIS Lady's mantle
Rounded leaves, lovely when wet, for each holds a glistening pearl of moisture at its centre. Sprays of lacy green flowers in summer, though the plant is attractive from spring to autumn. A free seeder.
HEIGHT 30cm (12in). CULTIVATION Sun or part-shade. Any soil. PROPAGATION Seed. HARDINESS 4.

ALSTROEMERIA LIGTU Princess lily
Rosy-pink to reddish blooms in umbels above blue-grey foliage in early summer.
HEIGHT 45–90cm (18in–3ft). CULTIVATION Sun. Rich, free-draining soil. PROPAGATION Easy from seed, but the roots resent disturbance. HARDINESS 4.

ANAPHALIS MARGARITACEA
Pearl everlasting
White, felty foliage and silvery everlasting flowers, each with a yellow centre, summer.
HEIGHT 30cm (3ft). CULTIVATION Sun. Any soil. PROPAGATION division. HARDINESS 4.

ANEMONE X HYBRIDA
Japanese anemone
Tall, spreading plants, soon making wide colonies, flowering in late summer.
HEIGHT 45–120cm (18in–4ft). CULTIVATION Sun. Any soil. PROPAGATION Division. HARDINESS 4.
'Honorine Jobert' Shapely single white blooms with bold golden stamens.
A. hupehensis 'September Charm' Related, but grows shorter (60cm/2ft), with delicate pink flowers.

AQUILEGIA Columbine
Attractive 'granny's bonnet'-shaped flowers in spring or early summer.
HEIGHT 45–90cm (18in–3ft). CULTIVATION Sun or part-shade. Rich soil. PROPAGATION Seed or division. HARDINESS 4.
A. alpina 'Hensol Harebell' Shapely blue flowers above glaucous, lobed foliage, spring.
A. vulgaris Many fine forms including 'Adelaide Addison' (blue and white), 'Magpie' (dark purple and white) and 'Crimson Star'.

ARGYRANTHEMUM Marguerite
Shrubby perennials often grown as annuals in pots; daisy-like summer flowers.
HEIGHT 45–90cm (18in–3ft). CULTIVATION Sun. Rich soil. PROPAGATION Cuttings. HARDINESS 2.

AQUILEGIA 'MAGPIE'

A. gracile 'Chelsea Girl' Lacy, filigree grey-green foliage and single white daisy flowers with yellow centres.
A. frutescens 'Jamaica Primrose' Feathery foliage, soft yellow blooms; 'Vancouver' pink.

ARTEMISIA Wormwood
Silvery-leaved perennials grown for their delicate foliage which enhances the garden from spring to autumn.
HEIGHT 45cm (18in). CULTIVATION Sun. Free-draining soil. Cut back to keep young. PROPAGATION cuttings. HARDINESS 4.

A. absinthium 'Lambrook Silver' The most finely divided and most silver of all the filigree artemisias.

A. ludoviciana Flannel-like leaves, almost white, on stems from a creeping rootstock.

ARUM ITALICUM 'MARMORATUM'

Marbled foliage emerges in autumn and persists through winter; tall, pale green spathes in spring lead to vivid red fruits in late summer and early autumn.

HEIGHT 25–45cm (10–18in). Spring, autumn, winter. CULTIVATION Sun or part-shade. Rich soil. PROPAGATION Seed or division. HARDINESS 4.

ASTER

A widely varied family of perennial plants flowering in summer and autumn.

HEIGHT 20–120cm (8in–4ft). CULTIVATION Sun. Rich soil, not too dry. PROPAGATION Division. HARDINESS 4.

A. amellus Early blooming on somewhat lax stems. Cultivars include '**King George**' (blue) and '**Pink Zenith**'.

A. x *frikartii* '**Mönch**' Late-summer-blooming aster with soft blue flowers and greenish-yellow centres.

A. lateriflorus '**Horizontalis**' Late-blooming, with a myriad tiny starry flowers in palest grey-pink, each with a darker pink centre, which persists until the beginning of winter.

A. novi-angliae '**Harrington's Pink**' Early autumn-flowering, tall growing, unique pale pink; '**Alma Pötschke**' is a more vivid cerise; '**Herbstschnee**' is white.

ASTRANTIA Melancholy gentleman

Distinctive perennials with crown-shaped flowers in summer.

HEIGHT 45–60cm (18–24in). CULTIVATION Sun or part-shade. PROPAGATION Seed or division. HARDINESS 4.

A. major Green and white crown-shaped

flowers with ragged edges; good forms include '**Shaggy**' and the maroon-flowered '**Hadspen Blood**'.

A. maxima Pink, crown-shaped flowers; needs a moist site.

BERGENIA

A large tribe of evergreen plants with coarse, often ruffled, leathery foliage and sprays of pink, lilac or white blooms in late winter to early spring. Good garden hybrids include 'Silberlicht' whose flowers are white and 'Abendglut' whose leaves are ruddy and whose semi-double flowers are a startling purplish-pink.

HEIGHT 30–45cm (12–18in). CULTIVATION Sun or part-shade. Any soil. PROPAGATION Division. HARDINESS 4.

B. purpurascens Has foliage colours well into winter.

BIDENS FERULIFOLIA

Trailing, tender plant with golden-yellow blooms produced throughout the growing season. Ideal for container use.

HEIGHT 45cm (18in). CULTIVATION Sun. Rich soil. PROPAGATION Seed, cuttings or division. HARDINESS 3.

***BERGENIA* 'ABENDGLUT'**

BRUNNERA MACROPHYLLA

Heart-shaped or rounded leaves and misty sprays of forget-me-not flowers in spring.

HEIGHT 30–45cm (12–18in) CULTIVATION Shade. Leafy soil. PROPAGATION Seed or division. HARDINESS 4.

'**Hadspen Cream**' A variegated form.

CAMPANULA Bellflower

C. lactiflora **Robust plants with soft green foliage and generous, long-lasting sprays of soft blue bell-shaped flowers in summer.**

HEIGHT 60–120cm (2–4ft). CULTIVATION Sun or part-shade. Rich soil. PROPAGATION Seed, division or root cuttings. HARDINESS 4.

'**Loddon Anna**' Pinkish flowers.

C. latiloba **Clusters of basal rosettes form a spring flower spike.**

HEIGHT 45–90cm (18in–3ft). CULTIVATION Sun or part-shade. Rich soil. PROPAGATION Seed or division. HARDINESS 4.

'**Percy Piper**' A good form with deep blue flowers. '**Hidcote Amethyst**' Carries relatively open flowers in soft mauve.

CATANANCHE CAERULEA

Bright blue flowers with papery sepals produced in succession all summer.

HEIGHT 45cm (18in) CULTIVATION Sun. Rich soil. PROPAGATION Seed or division. HARDINESS 4.

CENTRANTHUS RUBER Red valerian

Glaucous foliage and big panicles of flowers produced in spring and summer in three main colours: white, brick red and a rather flat purple-pink. Cut hard back after flowering to promote subsequent flushes of bloom. Will seed at will, with wind-borne seeds, so best prevented from setting too much seed anyway.

HEIGHT 45–60cm (18–24in). CULTIVATION Sun. Poor soil. PROPAGATION Seed. HARDINESS 4.

CHAEROPHYLLUM HIRSUTUM 'ROSEUM'

Ferny foliage in spring, with pink, Queen-Anne's-lace flowers in summer. Works well with late-spring bulbs.
HEIGHT 45–90cm (18in–3ft). CULTIVATION Part-shade. Any soil. PROPAGATION Division. HARDINESS 4.

CIMICIFUGA SIMPLEX 'ELSTEAD'

Divided foliage with rat-tail autumn flowers, dark in bud, opening creamy-white.
HEIGHT 45–120cm (18in–4ft). CULTIVATION Part-shade. Rich soil. PROPAGATION Seed or division. HARDINESS 4.

CONVALLARIA MAJALIS

Lily-of-the-valley
Fragrant, rounded, pearl-like white flowers among the broad foliage. Red berries sometimes produced in autumn.
HEIGHT 20cm (8in), spreading.
CULTIVATION Shade or part-shade. Any soil. PROPAGATION Division. HARDINESS 4.

CORTADERIA SELLOANA Pampas grass
Rustling, razor-sharp grass blades; silky flowerheads appear in late summer and last through winter. 'Pumila' is the only compact species, though still quite large, and therefore dramatic for a small garden.
HEIGHT 1.2–2m (4–6ft). CULTIVATION Sun or part-shade. Rich soil. PROPAGATION Seed or division. HARDINESS 4.

CRAMBE MARITIMA Seakale
Edible, undulating grey-green foliage, highly decorative when young, is joined by creamy-white, honey-scented flowers in summer. Happy even in salty seaside conditions.
HEIGHT 45cm (18in). CULTIVATION Sun. Any soil. PROPAGATION Seed or root cuttings. HARDINESS 4.

CROCOSMIA

African members of the gladiolus family growing from colonies of corms. Flowers in late summer and autumn, colours are often vivid red or orange.
HEIGHT 45–90cm (18in–3ft). CULTIVATION Sun. Free-draining soil but not too dry. PROPAGATION Division. HARDINESS 3/4. 'Lucifer' Brilliant red flowers among sword-like foliage in summer. 'Solfaterre' Khaki foliage, amber-yellow flowers; needs winter protection in cold area.

DAHLIA 'BISHOP OF LLANDAFF'

Dark, almost black foliage; burning scarlet blooms in late summer and autumn.
HEIGHT 45–90cm (18in–3ft). CULTIVATION Sun. Rich soil. PROPAGATION Division. HARDINESS 3.

DELPHINIUM BELLADONNA HYBRIDS

The most long-lasting of the classic delphiniums, producing generous numbers of flower spikes per plant in summer, and needing less support than do larger cultivars. Colours run through most of the blues and white. Divide regularly to ensure young, vigorous plants.
HEIGHT 60–120cm (2–4ft). CULTIVATION Sun. Rich soil. PROPAGATION Division or basal cuttings. HARDINESS 4.

DENDRANTHEMA 'MEI-KYO'

Chrysanthemum
Rugged, twiggy growth results in plants with a shrub-like appearance, covered with purplish-pink button flowers from mid-autumn onwards. Sports include 'Bronze Elegance' and the bright yellow 'Nantyderry Sunshine'.
HEIGHT 45cm (18in). CULTIVATION Sun. Rich soil. PROPAGATION Division or cuttings. HARDINESS 4.

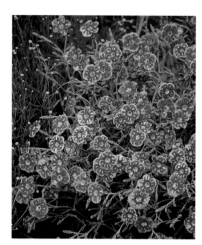

DIANTHUS CAESIUS

DIANTHUS Pinks and carnations
Within this varied and familiar family of plants, border pinks and alpine pinks are the best for small gardens.
HEIGHT 10–45cm (4–18in). CULTIVATION Sun. Well-drained, chalky soil. PROPAGATION Cuttings or seed. HARDINESS 3.
'Doris' One of the most regular to bloom, with salmon and carmine scented flowers. 'Haytor' Pinkish white. 'Dad's Favourite' Maroon-laced flowers.

DICENTRA

Finely divided ferny foliage, often galucous or purple-tinged, among which curiously shaped flowers appear in spring. Colours range from white through pinks to purple.
HEIGHT 45cm (18in). CULTIVATION Sun or light shade. Any soil. PROPAGATION Division. HARDINESS 4.
D. formosa Deeply cut and lobed foliage with generous numbers of pink, nodding bell-like flowers in spring and summer. *D.* 'Boothman's Variety' Darker leaves, wine-red flowers in spring. *D.* 'Langtrees' Flowers almost white. *D. spectabilis* A Chinese native, taller at 60cm (2ft), with large, intricate flowers in ivory and pink. 'Alba' Pure white flowers.

DORONICUM Leopard's bane

Spring flowers from the Alpine meadows of Europe, with sunshine colours and good stature for so early in the year.

HEIGHT 45cm (18in). CULTIVATION Sun or part-shade. Any soil. PROPAGATION Division. HARDINESS 4.

'**Miss Mason**' Bright yellow daisy flowers in mid-spring; exciting with red tulips.

'**Spring Beauty**' A dwarf form, with double golden flowers.

EPIMEDIUM

Durable foliage borne on wiry stems; leaves attactive, some more or less heart-shaped, and usually well-coloured; delicate flowers in soft colours to white appear above the foliage in spring.

HEIGHT 25–45cm (10–18in). CULTIVATION Part-shade. Leafy soil, not too dry but not boggy. PROPAGATION Division. HARDINESS 4.

E. x *rubrum* Ruby-red flowers, each with a white stripe running through the petals, followed by rusty foliage which lasts all summer and persists, after it has browned, through winter.

E. x *versicolor* 'Sulphureum' Pale yellow flowers, followed by well-marked young foliage which greens up for summer but turns russet again in autumn.

ERYSIMUM Perennial wallflower

A group of valuable, shrubby, spring-flowering plants which last for several years but need to be reproduced every second season to be sure of continuity.

HEIGHT 30–45cm (12–18in). CULTIVATION Sun. Free-draining soil. PROPAGATION Cuttings. HARDINESS 4.

'**Bowles' Mauve**' Greyish foliage and rich purple flowers, produced for most of spring. '**Chelsea Jacket**' More compact, with bronze cast to the foliage in frost. '**Harpur Crewe**' Double yellow, intensely fragrant blooms.

EUPHORBIA CHARACIAS

EUPHORBIA Spurge

E. characias **Big shrubby species, variable in appearance, usually with golden-green oblong flower spikes from spring to autumn. Subspecies** *E. c. wulfenii* **is more gold in flower colour than most, with wider, longer flowerheads.**

HEIGHT 1–1.2m (3–4ft). CULTIVATION Sun. Poor soil. PROPAGATION Seed. HARDINESS 4.

E. dulcis 'Chameleon' **Dark, coppery foliage and greenish flowers make a modestly beautiful plant, ideal for placing below shrubs or trees.**

HEIGHT 45cm (18in). CULTIVATION Part-shade. Any soil. PROPAGATION Seed or division. HARDINESS 4.

E. griffithii 'Dixter' **Fiery bracts and golden spring and summer flowers on this compact form make it the ideal choice for small gardens.**

HEIGHT 45cm (18in), spreading. CULTIVATION Part-shade. Any soil. PROPAGATION Division. HARDINESS 4.

E. palustris **Gives a vivid golden display all spring, followed by even richer colour in autumn.**

HEIGHT 1–1.2m (3–4ft). CULTIVATION Sun or part-shade. Rich or moist soil. PROPAGATION Division. HARDINESS 4.

FELICIA AMELLOIDES

Blue daisy flowers produced throughout the growing season, on pendulous plants, make this a fine choice for container use.

HEIGHT 45cm (18in). CULTIVATION Sun. Any soil. PROPAGATION Cuttings. HARDINESS 2.

FOENICULUM VULGARE 'PURPUREUM' Fennel

Huge growths of soft, feathery foliage in sombre bronze, particularly dark when young, through spring and summer. Greenish-yellow blooms are best removed before they mature, since seeding can be a problem. The green form is desirable, but less dramatic; both good as culinary herbs.

HEIGHT 60cm–1.6m (2–5ft). CULTIVATION Sun. Any soil. PROPAGATION Seed. HARDINESS 4.

GAURA LINDHEIMERI

Waving sprays of ephemeral white flowers which open each day for most of summer. A graceful front-of-border plant. Not hardy in cold areas.

HEIGHT 45–90cm (18in–3ft). CULTIVATION Sun. Any soil. PROPAGATION Division. HARDINESS 3.

GAZANIA KREBSIANA

Daisy flowers in summer in colours which burn like embers among the low grasses of their native South Africa. Excellent for bedding or for dotting in a summer border.

HEIGHT 15–25cm (6–8in). CULTIVATION Sun. Any warm soil. PROPAGATION Seed. HARDINESS 2.

GERANIUM Cranesbill

Graceful, elegant and long-flowering, mainly in blues and pinks. Sharp-pointed seed capsules resembling a bird's beak. Many spreading or clump-forming.

HEIGHT 25–90cm (8in–3ft). CULTIVATION Sun or part-shade. Any soil. PROPAGATION Division. HARDINESS 4.

G. x *cantabrigiense* 'Biokovo' Low-growing, with pinkish-white flowers and foliage that smells of ripe apples; makes good ground cover. 'Johnson's Blue' Large blue flowers above divided foliage on low-growing (25cm/10in) plants.

G. *pratense* Meadow cranesbill. Up to 1m (3ft) tall, with successions of blue flowers; white forms are also common. 'Mrs Kendall Clark' Pale blue variety with pearly flowers, made even prettier by darker striations.

G. *sanguineum* Bloody cranesbill. Low-growing, constantly flowering with dark rose-magenta blooms. Light pink G. *striatum* is closely related; 'Album' white form.

G. *wallichianum* 'Buxton's Variety' Sky-blue flowers with white centres in late summer on trailing stems.

GEUM RIVALE Wild water avens

Relative of the rose growing on spreading rhizomes with lobed, somewhat furry foliage and 5-petalled flowers, mostly in warm colours, with central stamens.

HEIGHT 20–45cm (8–18in). CULTIVATION Sun or part-shade. Any soil, not too dry. PROPAGATION Division. HARDINESS 4.
'Leonard's Variety' Coppery pink. 'Lionel Cox' Creamy-yellow with a dash of green.

HAKONECHLOA MACRA 'AUREOLA'

Low-growing grass with golden striped foliage from spring to autumn. Pendulous habit makes it good for container culture.
HEIGHT 25–45cm (10–18in). CULTIVATION Sun or part-shade. Good soil.
PROPAGATION Division. HARDINESS 4.

HELICHRYSUM PETIOLARE

Silver-leaved trailing plant with round, felted foliage for container use.

GERANIUM SANGUINEUM

CULTIVATION Sun. Any soil. PROPAGATION Cuttings. HARDINESS 3.

H. *splendidum* Silvery shrub with tiny yellow button flowers.

HELICTOTRICHON SEMPERVIRENS

Stately grass with narrow, sage green foliage and tall, waving flowers in summer.
HEIGHT 60–90cm (2–3ft). CULTIVATION Sun or part-shade. Good soil, not too dry.
PROPAGATION Division; seed. HARDINESS 4.

HELLEBORUS Hellebore

Winter-flowering members of the buttercup family with large, regular-shaped blooms, greenish with spots or suffusions of other colours.
HEIGHT 30–60cm (1–2ft). CULTIVATION Sun or part-shade. Any soil. PROPAGATION Division or seed. HARDINESS 4.

H. *argutifolius* Corsican native with prickly foliage and apple-green blooms; tall species.

H. *niger* Christmas rose. Low-growing, white flowers; needs richer soil than most.

H. *orientalis* hybrids Various species have been used to develop a colour range from white or pale green, through pinks and purples to near-black. Many of the blooms are netted and spotted.

HEMEROCALLIS Day lily

Many day lilies are too coarse for small gardens but H. *multiflora* 'Corky' produces an endless succession of cheerful yellow blooms on plants with narrow leaves.
H. *flava* is worth growing for the elegant, curved shapes of the yellow flowers and for their fragrance.
HEIGHT 60–90cm (2–3ft). CULTIVATION Sun or part-shade. Rich soil. PROPAGATION Division. HARDINESS 4.

HOSTA Plantain lily

Handsome foliage plants beloved of garden gurus and the subject of intensive breeding. In most gardens disfigured by slugs, unless precautions are taken or unless grown in containers set in sharp gravel over which slugs hate to creep.
HEIGHT 10–60cm (4in–2ft). CULTIVATION Part-shade. Moist soil. PROPAGATION Division. HARDINESS 4.

H. *fortunei* var. *albopicta* Two-tone variegated – lime green and dark green – but the leaves lose their interesting coloration by midsummer.

H. 'Honeybells' Green, undulating leaves; pale lilac-white flowers. Easy, dependable.

H. *sieboldiana* 'Blue Angel' Broad, glaucous foliage, deeply veined, keeps its colour all summer. Pale lilac blooms.

H. 'Snowden' Huge and architectural, in a small garden, its wide, pale glaucous leaves held almost horizontal as they mature.

IRIS *(see also Alpines)*

Strap-shaped foliage, uniquely tripartite flowers in a wide range of shapes, sizes and colours. Short-lived but exquisite in bloom. Many have an architectural quality.
I. *germanica* Tall bearded irises with hundreds of notable varieties. Large flowers on long stems in a multitude of colours for a short season in early summer. 'Blue

IRIS FOETIDISSIMA

Luster', 'Frost and Flame' (white with orange beard), 'Wabash', white and royal-purple bicolours) and 'Blue Shimmer' with creamy-white falls edged in blue picotee. HEIGHT 60–90cm (2–3ft). CULTIVATION Sun. Free-draining soil. PROPAGATION Division. HARDINESS 4.

I. foetidissima Stinking iris. Evergreen, beardless iris ideal for bog or water garden. Yellow or dull purple flowers, early summer; seedpods open to reveal rounded scarlet fruits which persist throughout winter. HEIGHT 30–60cm (1–2ft). CULTIVATION Sun or shade. Moist soil. PROPAGATION Division. HARDINESS 4.

I. sibirica Siberian iris. Tall plants with luxuriant foliage and several flowers per stem, mainly dark blue, purple-blue, white. HEIGHT 60–90cm (2–3ft). CULTIVATION Sun or shade. Moist soil. PROPAGATION Division. HARDINESS 4.

LAMIUM MACULATUM 'WHITE NANCY'

Green-edged, silver foliage and white dead-nettle flowers make this a choice ground cover for spring and summer. HEIGHT 25–60cm (10in–2ft). CULTIVATION Sun or shade. Any soil. PROPAGATION Division or cuttings. HARDINESS 4.
'Beacon Silver' Similar but with pink flowers; can become invasive in fertile soil.

LATHYRUS VERNUS

Vivid magenta pea-flowers on low-growing plants in early spring. HEIGHT 25–30cm (10–12in). CULTIVATION Sun. Any soil. PROPAGATION Division or seed; most seedlings will be true to the parent. HARDINESS 4.
'Alboroseus' Pale pink; 'Cyaneus' deep blue.

MECONOPSIS

Genus includes blue Himalayan poppies. Purest blue petals, offset by golden-yellow centres above bristling foliage. HEIGHT 25–60cm (2–3ft). CULTIVATION Shade. Leafy soil. PROPAGATION Division or seed. HARDINESS 4.
M. betonicifolia Easiest to raise from seed and produces somewhat ruffled, sky-blue flowers – lavender-blue on limy soils.
M. grandis Larger flowers which hang gracefully and which retain their pure blue colour whatever the soil type.

NEMESIA CAERULEA

Pale lavender flowers, with a fragrance similar to that of heliotrope, in constant supply during spring and summer. Needs winter protection. HEIGHT 25–60cm (10in–2ft). CULTIVATION Sun. Any soil. PROPAGATION Division or cuttings. HARDINESS 3.

OSTEOSPERMUM

South African daisies open in sunshine to reveal bright insides which contrast with their duller coloured petal-backs. HEIGHT 30–60cm (1–2ft). CULTIVATION Sun. Free-draining soil. PROPAGATION Cuttings. HARDINESS 3.
O. 'Buttermilk' Beige outside, soft beige to straw yellow within; dark flower centres.
O. *jucundum* White or soft pink flowers. 'Lady Leitrim' Pink flowers. 'Pink Whirls' Spoon-shaped florets.

PELARGONIUM

A huge and valuable group of summer-flowering and foliage plants, tender but easily propagated. Fragrant kinds include 'Chocolate Peppermint', the musky smelling *P. quercifolium* and the sweetly spicy *P. fragrans*. Other outstanding varieties are mentioned below. HEIGHT 15–90cm (6in–3ft). CULTIVATION Sun. Free-draining soil. PROPAGATION Cuttings or seed. HARDINESS 2/3.
'Angel Series' Compact regal pelargoniums, ideal for containers, in bright clean colours.
P. peltatum The ivy-leaved trailing plants. 'Balcon series' are fine examples, as is the old but redoubtable variegated 'L'Elégante'. *P. zonale* Traditional 'pot geraniums'. Such seed-raised series as 'Orbit' now compete with cuttings-raised kinds like 'Frank Headley' or 'Dolly Varden' which contribute foliage as well as flower. 'The Boar' has a semi-trailing habit, single salmon flowers and bold black marks on its foliage.

PENSTEMON

The herbaceous kinds are in flower for so long and come in such a range of colours as to be almost indispensable. The larger the leaves, the less hardy they are, but it is advisable to take cuttings of all for overwintering under glass, since no species is totally hardy in sustained, severe frost. HEIGHT 30–60cm (1–2ft). CULTIVATION Sun. Free-draining, fertile soil. PROPAGATION Cuttings. HARDINESS 3/4.
P. 'Apple Blossom' Pink-flowered.
P. 'Evelyn' Exceptionally tough, small-leaved, pink-flowered.

P. 'Garnet' Wine-coloured flowers.
P. hartwegii Scarlet flowers.
P. 'Alice Hindley' Tender, with foxglove-sized blooms in soft lilac with white throats.
P. 'Stapleford Gem' Smaller, deeper purple and white.

PHLOMIS RUSSELIANA
Tall plants with somewhat felty leaves and pale ochre flowers produced in whorls along the stems in summer and autumn.
HEIGHT 60–90cm (2–3ft). CULTIVATION Sun or light shade. Free-draining soil. PROPAGATION Cuttings; seed. HARDINESS 4.

PHYGELIUS AEQUALIS
Damp-loving plants with successions of tubular flowers, salmon red on the outsides with contrasting yellow centres, summer.
HEIGHT 60–90cm (2–3ft). CULTIVATION Sun or shade. Moist, fertile soil. PROPAGATION Cuttings or division. HARDINESS 4.
'Yellow Trumpet' Flowers primrose yellow.

POLEMONIUM Jacob's ladder
Foliage reminiscent of primitive ladders, among which flowers, mostly blue with

POLYGONATUM X HYBRIDUM

bright yellow stamens, lodge like gems.
HEIGHT 30–60cm (1–2ft). CULTIVATION Sun. Free-draining soil. PROPAGATION Division or seed. HARDINESS 4.
P. 'Lambrook Mauve' A non-invasive hybrid to 30cm (1ft), soft lilac blooms.

POLYGONATUM Solomon's seal
Woodland plants with creeping rootstock and arching stems underhung with bell-shaped blooms. Some species are fragrant.
HEIGHT 60cm (2ft). CULTIVATION Shade. Any soil. PROPAGATION Division. HARDINESS 4.
P. x *hybridum* Best garden form resulting from American/European cross. White flowers held below arching stems, one cluster at each leaf joint.
P. odoratum A smaller, European species with stems less than 45cm (18in) long, better at coping with dry shade.

PRIMULA (*see also Alpines*)
Asiatic primulas bring a dash of bright summer colour to moist shade or they can be grown as bog plants.
HEIGHT 30–60cm (1–2ft). CULTIVATION Sun or dappled shade. Moist soil. PROPAGATION Seed. HARDINESS 4.
P. florindae Single heads, dusty in bud, with fragrant yellow blooms like huge cowslips.
P. japonica Wine red, candelabra-like blooms, with flowers in a series of whorls.
P. bulleyana Similar, with orange flowers.

SEDUM
Fleshy, often darkened foliage provides summer interest, followed in late summer to autumn by flat-topped inflorescences in ruby, pale pink or yellow shades.
HEIGHT 30–60cm (1–2ft). CULTIVATION Sun. Any soil. PROPAGATION Division. HARDINESS 4.
S. spectabile Ice plant. Cool green foliage

and pink blooms. 'Brilliant' or the darker pink 'Herbstfreude' are the best cultivars.
S. telephium Creamy or rusty flowers in autumn. subsp. *maximum* 'Atropurpureum' Outstanding foliage.
S. 'Vera Jameson' Dusky foliage and sulky purple to pink flowers.
S. 'Bertram Anderson' Foliage so dark as to be almost black when young; purple-red flowers in midsummer.

SEDUM 'HERBSTFREUDE'

SMILACINA RACEMOSA
Similar to Solomon's seal but spring flowers produced in creamy tufts at the stem ends.
HEIGHT 60cm (2ft). CULTIVATION Shade. Moist soil. PROPAGATION Division. HARDINESS 4.

TRICYRTIS FORMOSANA Toad lily
Glossy foliage with intriguing purple to brown flowers spotted with white, autumn.
HEIGHT 60–90cm (2–3ft). CULTIVATION Sun or dappled shade. Moist soil. PROPAGATION Division. HARDINESS 4.

TRILLIUM GRANDIFLORUM
Three-petalled white flowers above three broad leaves on a single stem, in spring.
HEIGHT 30cm (1ft), spreading. CULTIVATION Shade. Moist soil, preferably lime-free. PROPAGATION Seed or division. HARDINESS 4.

SHRUBS

Sizes in this group are given as:
Small (less than 60cm/2ft high);
Medium (up to 1m/3ft 3in); Large (up to
2.5m/8ft). Propagation is by cuttings unless
otherwise stated.

ABUTILON

**Members of the mallow family, valuable
for their bold foliage and summer flowers
whose red, yellow or pastel-coloured petals
surround a fused central spike of stamens.**
HEIGHT Medium. CULTIVATION Sun or
dappled shade. Any soil. HARDINESS 3.
A. 'Ashford Red'; *A.* 'Canary Bird' Yellow.
A. x *suntense* Vine-like foliage and pale
mauve to blue flowers all summer. Fine
when freestanding or trained as a wall plant.
Needs protection from heavy frost.

ARTEMISIA

**Family of small-growing evergreen shrubs
with interesting foliage.**
HEIGHT Small. CULTIVATION Sun. Any
free-draining soil. HARDINESS 4.
A. abrotanum Lad's love. Strongly
aromatic; green, lacy foliage and dark stems.
A. 'Powis Castle' Silvery filigree foliage on
scrubby plants; best pinched back regularly
to keep them stocky and leafy.

AUCUBA JAPONICA

**Durable evergreens with sea-green stems
and waxy foliage. Females bear red berries.**
HEIGHT Medium/large. CULTIVATION Shade
or dappled shade. Any soil. HARDINESS 4.
"Crotonifolia' Cream-stippled leaves.
Picturata' Foliage boldly cream-splashed.

BERBERIS

**Small-leaved, mostly evergreen shrubs
with small flowers and, later, fruit.**
HEIGHT Medium to large. CULTIVATION

Sun, dappled shade. Any soil. HARDINESS 4.
B. darwinii Evergreen with three-pointed
leaves, yellow flowers in spring, followed by
blue-black berries.
B. x *stenophylla* Evergreen with slender,
arching branches; golden spring flowers.
B. thunbergii 'Atropurpurea Nana' Small,
purple foliage which colours well in autumn.

BRACHYGLOTTIS GREYI

**Low-growing evergreen with oval, dark
green leaves with grey backs and sunshine-
yellow daisy flowers. (Formerly known as
Senecio.)**
HEIGHT Small. CULTIVATION Sun. Free-
draining soil. HARDINESS 3/4.

AUCUBA JAPONICA 'CROTONIFOLIA'

BUDDLEJA DAVIDII Butterfly bush
Fragrant pink flower panicles, late summer.
HEIGHT Large; better if cut back each year.
CULTIVATION Sun. Any soil. HARDINESS 4.
'Black Knight' has the darkest flowers.
'Lochinch' A fine hybrid; smoky-grey leaves.

BUXUS SEMPERVIRENS Box
**Slow-growing, small-leaved shrub, perfect
for small hedges; can be clipped to any size.**
HEIGHT Small. CULTIVATION Sun or shade.
any soil. HARDINESS 4.
'Suffruticosa' The most compact variety.

CAMELLIA x WILLIAMSII

**Within a massive genus of evergreen
shrubs, this group is of great value for
small gardens since they flower through
winter and are exceptionally hardy.**
HEIGHT Medium to large. CULTIVATION
Shade or dappled shade. Any lime-free soil.
'Donation' Semi-double, pink flowers with
darker veining through the petals. 'J.C.
Williams' A single, clean pink flowers.

CEANOTHUS

**Though many are sensitive to frost, these
make fine shrubs, with their fluffy blue
flowers, especially if trained on a sheltered
wall. Some are evergreen.**
HEIGHT Medium to large or low and
spreading. CULTIVATION Sun. Any soil.
HARDINESS 3/4.
C. 'Autumnal Blue' A tough evergreen
hybrid, flowering in late summer.

CERATOSTIGMA
PLUMBAGINOIDES

**Vivid blue flowers appear in midsummer
and continue through autumn, when the
foliage turns red. Cut hard back each
spring to ensure plentiful blooms.**
HEIGHT Small. CULTIVATION Sun. Any soil.
HARDINESS 4.

CHAENOMELES Japanese quince
**A superb wall shrub, bearing edible fruit in
autumn and richly coloured blossom in late
winter and spring.**
HEIGHT Medium to large. CULTIVATION Sun
or dappled shade. Any soil. HARDINESS 4.
C. speciosa 'Moerloosei' Greenish-pink
and white blossoms.
C. superba 'Crimson and Gold' Makes a
contrast between the gold stamens and
startling petals. 'Pink Lady' Shell-pink
flowers, produced in a generous flush in
early spring.

CISTUS Rock rose

Lovers of hot, arid conditions, the rock rose flowers last only a day but are produced over several weeks, in early summer, and make a vivid display.
HEIGHT Small to medium. CULTIVATION Sun. Any free-draining soil. HARDINESS 4.
C. ladanifer Glutinous foliage, with musky odour, and large white flowers.
C. laurifolius Evergreen; white flowers with yellow centres.

CORDYLINE AUSTRALIS

Spiky evergreen foliage and, eventually, gawky, naked stems and fragrant flowers. Useful in containers or as a focal plant for formal gardening. Besides green, there are bronze- and red-leaved forms.
HEIGHT Large. CULTIVATION Sun. Any soil. HARDINESS 3.

CORNUS Dogwood

Excellent shrubs for clipping hard back each spring (pollarding) to produce forests of young, colourful wands.
HEIGHT Medium. CULTIVATION Sun or dappled shade. Any soil but not too dry.

CORNUS ALBA 'SIBIRICA'

HARDINESS 4.
C. alba 'Aurea' Gold foliage and red stems.
'Elegantissima' Cream-variegated foliage.
'Sibirica' Vivid red stems.
C. mas Cornelian cherry. Tiny yellow flowers in winter; good summer foliage; rich autumn colour. 'Variegata' White and green foliage; superb autumn colouring.
C. stolonifera 'Flavirama' With greenish-yellow stems.

CORONILLA VALENTINA GLAUCA

Vivid yellow pea-flowers produced constantly on lax evergreen shrubs which can be trained as wall plants. Prune hard in spring to stimulate fresh growth.
HEIGHT Small. CULTIVATION Sun. Any free-draining soil. HARDINESS 3.
'Citrina' Pale yellow flowers.

CORYLUS AVELLANA Hazel

Suckering shrubs with winter catkins and edible nuts; make a good winter outline. Effective seen against evergreens such as holly or laurel.
HEIGHT Medium to large. CULTIVATION Shade or sun. Any soil. HARDINESS 4.
'Contorta' Curiously contorted. 'Aurea' Gold-leaved form. 'Rubra' Red-leaved form.

COTONEASTER

One of the most valuable genera, not only for their autumn berries but for their foliage, habit and, in many, their attractive spring and summer flowers.
HEIGHT Medium and large. CULTIVATION Sun or dappled shade. Any soil. HARDINESS 4.
C. adpressus Small leaves, turning red in autumn; red berries.
C. conspicuus 'Decorus' Arching stems, white blossoms, red berries.
C. horizontalis Fishbone stems, red berries, good autumn colour. A perfect host wall plant for other climbers to weave through.

COTONEASTER

DAPHNE

Often short-lived, but choice shrubs, mainly valuable for the fragrance of their early-summer blooms.
HEIGHT Small. CULTIVATION Sun or dappled shade. Any soil, not too dry.
HARDINESS 4.
D. x *burkwoodii* Deciduous; heavy crop of richly fragrant, pink-backed white flowers.
D. tangutica Small, evergreen shrub with main flush of purple-backed, fragrant white flowers in spring, but further blossom through summer.

DEUTZIA x ELEGANTISSIMA 'ROSEALIND'

Rosy-pink flowers produced in profusion at the beginning of summer.
HEIGHT Medium. CULTIVATION Sun or dappled shade. Any soil. HARDINESS 4.

ELAEAGNUS x EBBINGEI

Evergreen shrub whose foliage holds interest all year round. Use as a hedge or a foil for more spectacular plants.
HEIGHT Medium to large. CULTIVATION Shade or dappled shade. Any soil.
HARDINESS 4.
'Gilt Edge' Vivid gold-variegated foliage, making an excellent background for red cornus twigs. 'Limelight' More muted variegations in lime green and dark green.

ERICA Heather

Among the most popular of groundcover shrubs, with colourful flowers at most times of year and, often, decorative foliage. Most are happiest in lime-free soil, but certain species are lime-tolerant and flower in winter, so are useful for small gardens. HEIGHT Small. CULTIVATION Sun. Any soil, but some species hate lime. HARDINESS 4.
E. carnea in variety. Lime-tolerant, winter-flowering in clean colours, mainly pink.
'Springwood White' The most dependable white form.

ESCALLONIA

Handsome evergreen shrubs, good for hedging in mild areas, with pink or white flowers through summer.
HEIGHT Medium to large. CULTIVATION Sun. Any soil. HARDINESS 4.
'Apple Blossom' Pale pink and white.
'Donard Star' A deeper pink.

FOTHERGILLA MAJOR

Creamy, feathery flowers in spring and superb red autumn foliage colour.
HEIGHT Small. CULTIVATION Shade or dappled shade. Lime-free soil. HARDINESS 4.

FREMONTODENDRON 'CALIFORNIA GLORY'

The finest cultivar of this vivid yellow-flowered evergreen shrub. Best grown on a warm wall in full sun. Stems and leaves carry a mealy substance which can irritate.
HEIGHT Medium to large. CULTIVATION Sun. Any soil. HARDINESS 4.

FUCHSIA MAGELLANICA

The hardiest species in a vast group of container and garden plants; often best grown from cuttings each year. Evergreen in mild areas. Narrow pendulous cherry-red tubular flowers with purple-blue centres.

HEIGHT Medium. CULTIVATION Sun or dappled shade. Any soil. HARDINESS 3.

GARRYA ELLIPTICA

Evergreen shrub made distinctive, in the male plant, by long catkins which extend in midwinter. In cold areas, prefers the protection of a wall.
HEIGHT Medium to large. CULTIVATION Shade or dappled shade. Any soil.
HARDINESS 4.
'James Roof' The clone to look for, with longer catkins.

GRISELINIA LITTORALIS

Excellent evergreen hedging plant for maritime regions but not fully frost hardy.
HEIGHT medium to large, but clippable to any size. CULTIVATION Sun or dappled shade. any soil. HARDINESS 3/4.

HAMAMELIS MOLLIS Witch hazel
Spidery, yellow, fragrant blooms in winter and superb russet, red and gold autumn foliage colour.
HEIGHT Medium, ultimately large.
CULTIVATION Sun or shade. Any soil but not too chalky. HARDINESS 4.

GARRYA ELLIPTICA 'JAMES ROOF'

HIPPOPHAE RHAMNOIDES

Sea buckthorn
Twiggy shrubs with silvery foliage and massed orange berries; good for the seaside.
HEIGHT Medium. CULTIVATION Sun. Any soil. HARDINESS 4.

HYDRANGEA

The mophead and lacecap hydrangeas provide colour for months on end, the bright blue and pink of their flowers gradually declining to green, maroon and ultimately buff as autumn advances.
HEIGHT Medium. CULTIVATION Shade or dappled shade. Any soil, not too dry.
HARDINESS 4.
H. macrophylla 'Ayesha' Soft lilac mopheads. 'Ami Pasquier' Deep, plummy red. 'Blue Wave' Blue lacecap variety.

HYPERICUM 'HIDCOTE' St John's wort
Brilliant golden flowers throughout the second half of summer on compact semi-evergreen shrubs, followed by red berries.
HEIGHT Medium. CULTIVATION Sun or dappled shade. Any soil. HARDINESS 4.

LAVANDULA Lavender
Aromatic evergreen shrubs with fragrant blooms in summer. Clip back, after main flowering, to ensure compact shrubs. Sporadic blooms produced in autumn.
HEIGHT Small. CULTIVATION Sun. Free-draining soil. HARDINESS 4.
H. angustifolia 'Hidcote' Dark purple blue flowers. 'Hidcote Pink' Pale lilac-pink blooms. 'Twickel Purple' A fine cultivar with purple blooms. 'Vera' Taller growing.

LAVATERA
A group of prolific, summer-flowering shrubs, mainly pink or white blooms.
HEIGHT Medium to large. CULTIVATION Sun. Any soil. HARDINESS 4 .

HYDRANGEA MACROPHYLLA 'AYESHA'

L. olbia 'Rosea' Large silvery-pink flowers produced in profusion all summer. Prune hard back in early spring for best results.
L. 'Barnsley' Carmine-centred white blooms which fade pink.

MAHONIA JAPONICA

Evergreen shrubs with holly-like foliage. Flowers, produced at the growing tips each winter, are soft primrose yellow and richly fragrant. Gawky habit makes this a companion shrub rather than a soloist.
HEIGHT Medium. CULTIVATION Shade or dappled shade. Any soil. HARDINESS 4.

PAEONIA SUFFRUTICOSA HYBRIDS

Grown for the impact of their huge showy flowers, though only in flower for a short spell in early summer. The divided foliage is attractive too. A real star performer.
HEIGHT Medium. CULTIVATION Sun. Rich soil. HARDINESS 4.

PHILADELPHUS Mock orange

Intensely fragrant white blooms beautify this shrub as spring melts into summer. Smaller, better behaved varieties include *P. coronarius* 'Variegatus' and gold *P. c.* 'Aureus'; both perform best in light shade.
HEIGHT Medium or large. CULTIVATION Shade, dappled shade or sun. Any soil. HARDINESS 4.

P. 'Manteau d'Hermine' Small, with double flowers.
P. 'Belle Etoile' Carries the largest flowers, strongly scented and with a maroon centre.

PHYSOCARPUS OPULIFOLIUS 'DART'S GOLD'

One of the most useful foliage shrubs for semi-shade, with reddish stems from which the bark peels. Luminous gold foliage in early spring, colouring well in autumn. Attractive winter outline.
HEIGHT Medium. CULTIVATION Shade or dappled shade. Any soil. HARDINESS 4.

PIERIS 'FOREST FLAME'

The spring and summer flowers are small and white, like lily-of-the-valley, but this evergreen plant's beauty also comes from its developing shoots, vivid red when young.
HEIGHT Small to medium. CULTIVATION shade or dappled shade. Lime-free soil.
HARDINESS 4.

PIPTANTHUS NEPALENSIS

This evergreen shrub has three-lobed, dark green foliage and bright yellow pea-flowers in spring. The green stems make it a good winter shrub, but it needs

MAHONIA JAPONICA

protection from sustained frost.
HEIGHT Medium. CULTIVATION Sun. Any soil. HARDINESS 3/4.

RHODODENDRON

A vast group of some excellent species and varieties, mostly evergreen. For small gardens, one must weigh up length of time out of bloom (on average, about 50 weeks) with the space occupied.
HEIGHT All sizes. CULTIVATION Shade or dappled shade. Lime-free soil, not too dry.
HARDINESS 4.
The best small or medium species are:
R. calostrotum 'Gigha' Intense red blooms in spring.
R. scintillans Shiny foliage, blue flowers.
R. yakushimanum Pretty foliage, with rusty meal on its undersides.
This group includes azaleas too: the most useful for small gardens are such evergreen hybrids as 'Betty' (pink) or 'Hinodegiri' (red).

ROSA (*see page 138*)

ROSMARINUS OFFICINALIS

Aromatic evergreen needle-like foliage, small blue-grey flowers in late winter to early spring. Prostrate forms of rosemary, such as 'Severn Sea', are less hardy and need winter protection.
HEIGHT Small. CULTIVATION Sun. Free-draining soil. HARDINESS 3/4.
'Miss Jessop's Upright' Good hedging form.

RUBUS COCKBURNIANUS 'GOLDEN VALE'

Vigorous suckering shrub with bright golden foliage, making a perfect foil for blue flowers. In winter, stems are covered in a glowing white to grey bloom.
HEIGHT Medium to large, but cut back hard each spring. CULTIVATION Sun or dappled shade. Any soil. HARDINESS 4.

ROSA Rose

OLD ROSES

Old roses, even those which do not repeat, are worth using for their exquisite fragrance and their soft colours. In period gardens particularly, old roses may well look more comfortable than modern bush roses. Old roses are classified in the following main groups: within each group suggestions are given of the most suitable varieties for small gardens.

ROSA GALLICA 'VERSICOLOR'

Rosa alba: 'Maiden's Blush' Palest pink, vigorous, to 1.5m (5ft).
Rosa gallica: *Rosa mundi* Two-tone pink-striped; 'Charles de Mills' crimson; both moderately vigorous, to 1.3m (4ft).
Damask roses: 'Ispahan' Pink, intensely fragrant, vigorous, to 2m (6ft), useful as a low climber.
Moss roses: 'Old Pink Moss' Low-growing to 1.2m (3ft 6in).
China roses: 'Cécile Brunner' Salmon buds; 'Perle d'Or' shell pink; both to 1m (3ft).
Rosa rugosa: 'Roseraie de l'Haÿ' Heady scent, purple blooms, vigorous to 2m (6ft).

CLIMBERS AND RAMBLERS

'Albertine' Medium-sized, salmon flowers, dark stems, vigorous.

ROSA 'LADY HILLINGDON'

'New Dawn' Soft pink flowers with clean fragrance, vigorous and recurrent.
'Lady Hillingdon' Large apricot flowers, dark stems, moderate vigour.
'Danse du Feu' Scarlet red, moderate vigour.
'Climbing Iceberg' Pure white flowers, great vigour but no scent.
'Scarlet Fire' Single blooms, opening scarlet, fading crimson, orange hips.
'Albéric Barbier' Lemon flowers, opening ivory-white, faint scent, superb, glossy foliage; one of the greatest of the climbers.
'Gloire de Dijon' Beige to yellow flowers, very double, recurrent.

LARGE-FLOWERED

(formerly hybrid teas)
'Peace' Peachy-lemon, suffused with pink, vigorous.
'Alec's Red' Good vigour and fragrance.
'Just Joey' Salmon flowers, excellent bedding.
'Blessings' Soft pink.
'Polar Star' Greenish-white.

CLUSTER-FLOWERED

(formerly floribundas)
'Iceberg' White, medium vigour, no scent.
'Flower Carpet' Pink, disease-resistant.
'Ingrid Bergman' Deep red, with well-formed buds.
'Greenall's Glory' Intriguing effect of pink layered on white.

PATIO ROSES

'Little Bo-Peep' and 'Pretty Polly' Both pink.
'Sweet Dream' Peachy.
'Festival' Red.

MODERN SHRUB ROSES

'Nevada' Large shrub with dark stems and creamy, semi-double blooms.
'Cérise Bouquet' Open habit, large, with shocking-pink blooms; this rose needs careful siting.
'Frühlingsgold' Large, open, semi-double blooms with pale yellow centres and pink edges.
'Stanwell Perpetual' Ferny foliage, double pinkish flowers fading white.

HYBRID MUSKS

These repeat-flowering, fragrant roses are good for autumn as well as summer colour if they are pruned in summer and fed generously.
'Prosperity' Lemon in the bud, opening white with a dash of pink as they fade.
'Buff Beauty' Apricot in bud, fading to peachy buff.

ROSA 'BUFF BEAUTY'

RUSCUS ACULEATUS

Quietly beautiful, rather than sensational, but this evergreen shrub tolerates shade and the female plants have attractive berries, making it a useful contributor.
HEIGHT Small. CULTIVATION Shade. Any soil. HARDINESS 4.

SALIX Willow

Only the less vigorous willows are suitable for small gardens, since in some species the roots can become invasive and cause damage to buildings and drains. Most willows have an attractive twiggy winter outline and catkins. Beautiful when underplanted with snowdrops or aconites.
HEIGHT Small, medium or large.
CULTIVATION Sun or dappled shade.
HARDINESS 4.
The following species are more gentle in their growth rate:
S. acutifolia Large shrub with silvery catkins in early spring. 'Blue Streak' Bluish-white stems in the winter if they are pollarded each spring.
S. arbuscula Tiny willow with a pendulous habit.
S. caprea 'Kilmarnock' Weeping form of goat willow, with good spring catkins.
S. gracilistyla 'Melanostachys' Medium shrub with black catkins.
S. lanata Silvery, felty foliage on dwarf, twiggy bushes.

SAMBUCUS NIGRA Elder

Suckering, vigorous shrub with showy flowers and autumn berries. Eventually large but trimmable: cut back to encourage young growths and larger leaves.
HEIGHT Large. CULTIVATION Shade or dappled shade. Any soil. HARDINESS 4.
'Guincho Purple' A dark-leaved form, with pink-flushed blossoms and black berries.
'Aurea' Gold-leaved. 'Laciniata' Lacy foliage.

SANTOLINA Cotton lavender

Compact bushes with convoluted grey foliage and lemon or mustard button flowers. Good for a low hedge. Inclined to sprawl with age.
HEIGHT Small. CULTIVATION Sun. Free-draining soil. HARDINESS 4.
S. pinnata 'Sulphurea' Aromatic grey foliage; lemon-yellow flowers in summer.
S. rosmarinifolia 'Primrose Gem' Darker green foliage, setting off the pale yellow button flowers to perfection.

SARCOCOCCA HOOKERIANA

Low evergreens with dark, glossy foliage and tiny off-white flowers, in winter, which smell strongly of honey. Makes a good spreading ground cover in dense shade.
HEIGHT Small. CULTIVATION Shade or dappled shade. any soil. HARDINESS 4.

VIBURNUM

Useful group of shrubs, some of which are evergreen. Fine in a general shrub border or freestanding as specimens.
HEIGHT Medium to large. CULTIVATION Sun, shade or dappled shade. Any soil.
HARDINESS 4.
V. carlcephalum Intensely fragrant, rounded white flowers in spring and early summer on large shrubs with an open habit.
V. farreri Autumn- and winter-flowering with very fragrant pale pink or white blooms.
V. plicatum 'Mariesii' Summer-flowering, the branches arranged in tiers with the flat-topped flowers along their lengths.
V. tinus 'Eve Price' Evergreen, winter- and spring-flowering with pink-tinged, white blooms. Good for hedging or freestanding.

VINCA Periwinkle

Evergreen ground-cover plants, which can be invasive but are good natured enough to thrive in dense shade, producing blue,

VIBURNUM PLICATUM 'MARIESII'

purple or white blooms in spring. Superb ground cover even under evergreen trees.
HEIGHT Small. CULTIVATION Shade or dappled shade. Any soil. HARDINESS 4.
V. minor Bright blue flowers and dark foliage. 'Gertrude Jekyll' White flowers. 'Atropurpurea' Magenta flowers. 'Argenteomarginata' Silver-edged leaves; one of several variegated forms.

WEIGELA FLORIDA

Pink or red flowers, produced in profusion in late spring. Coloured-leaf forms have the added advantage of a later display and frequently colour well in autumn, representing good value for small gardens.
HEIGHT Medium. CULTIVATION Sun and dappled shade. Any soil. HARDINESS 4.
'Variegata' Particularly effective, with its mid-pink blooms set off by creamy leaf margins; if pruned hard immediately after flowering, the resulting young stems carry larger than normal leaves.

YUCCA FILAMENTOSA

A compact form of the stately, exotic-looking genus with hairy filaments along the sides of the stiff, sword-like evergreen leaves in summer. The 1m (3ft) spires are thickly populated with cup-shaped cream flowers.
HEIGHT Small. CULTIVATION Sun. Any soil. HARDINESS 4.

TREES

Sizes in this group are given as:
Small (ultimate size less than 6m/20ft);
Medium (ultimate height less than
11m/36ft); Large (anything over 11m/36ft).

ACER

The acers are ornamental trees grown for their foliage (often with good autumn colour) and their outline. All the acers listed are happiest in conditions that imitate woodland floors, that is, shade, shelter from wind, not too cold. Most effective when their outline is seen in its entirety. Beautiful overhanging water.
HEIGHT Small. CULTIVATION Shade or dappled shade. Most soils, not too dry.
HARDINESS 4.
A. davidii 'George Forrest' Snakebark maple. Well-marked trunk, with streaks and veins; colours red and yellow in autumn.
A. japonicum 'Vitifolium' Golden-green, fan-shaped leaves, reminiscent of vine leaves. Spreading outline; superb autumn colour.
A. palmatum 'Bloodgood' A very small maple with black stems and dark foliage.
'Burgundy Lace' A form with deeply cut, reddish foliage.
'Dissectum' The most commonly grown form, with green, deeply laced foliage.

ACER PALMATUM 'DISSECTUM ATROPURPUREUM'

AESCULUS INDICA Indian chestnut
More refined than the familiar horse chestnut, with glossy, palmate leaves and a good outline. The blossom comes a month later in early summer. Fine choice for a medium to large lawn tree.
HEIGHT Medium. CULTIVATION Sun or dappled shade. Most soils. HARDINESS 4.

AMELANCHIER LAMARCKII
Showy white blossoms in spring, amid glossy emerging foliage. Red and gold autumn colour. Can be pruned to size.
HEIGHT Small to medium. CULTIVATION Sun or shade. Most soils. HARDINESS 4.

ARBUTUS UNEDO Strawberry tree
Small clusters of cream lantern-shaped flowers on this evergreen tree are followed by edible, roughened scarlet to orange fruits a little like strawberries. In mature plants, the trunk and branches are an interesting feature, carrying rust-coloured bark. Good outline.
HEIGHT Small. CULTIVATION Shade or dappled shade. Most soils, not too dry.
HARDINESS 4.

BETULA UTILIS JACQUEMONTII
The whitest of the birches, with snow-white trunk and main branches. Beautiful contrast between pale trunk and fresh young foliage. Good grown as a multi-trunked tree.
HEIGHT Large. CULTIVATION Sun, dappled shade. Most soils, not too dry. HARDINESS 4.

CARPINUS BETULUS 'FASTIGIATA'
The common hornbeam makes a fine hedging plant, particularly on heavy soil, but this upright form, with fresh green foliage and pretty, hanging green leafy 'fruits', has an outline that ultimately spreads to imitate that of a candle flame.
HEIGHT Large. CULTIVATION Sun, shade or dappled shade. Most soils. HARDINESS 4.

CRATAEGUS Hawthorn
Hawthorns are wildlife-friendly, having nourishing haws (fruits) and, as they mature, offering nesting sites.
HEIGHT Small or medium. CULTIVATION Sun. Most soils. HARDINESS 4.
C. laevigata 'Crimson Cloud' An ornamental variety with single red flowers and dull red fruits.
C. prunifolia Simple leaves, like those of a plum, with creamy flowers in late spring and golden-orange fruits in autumn.
C. tanacetifolia Small species with gnarled features, finely dissected foliage and creamy blossoms in summer.

EUCRYPHIA 'NYMANSAY'
Glossy, dark green foliage and white waxy blossoms in late summer make this a valuable tree but it needs shelter from the worst of the winter weather.
HEIGHT Medium CULTIIVATION Sun, shade or dappled shade. Most soils, not too dry.
HARDINESS 3/4.

FAGUS SYLVATICA Beech
'Dawyck Purple' and 'Dawyck Gold' are two upright forms of beech, with gold or purple foliage, providing good outline without stealing too much space.
HEIGHT Medium to large. CULTIVATION Sun. Most soils. HARDINESS 4.

ILEX Holly
This useful group of trees have much to offer small gardens int terms of their evergreen, often variegated, foliage and their shapely outline.
HEIGHT Small to medium (can be clipped to size). CULTIVATION Sun, shade or dappled shade. Most soils, not too dry. HARDINESS 4.

MALUS 'JOHN DOWNIE'

I. x *altaclerensis* 'Belgica Aurea' Large, oval leaves, gold-edged; red berries. 'Lawsoniana' Leaves streaked and flecked with gold and yellow.

I. aquifolium Almost all forms of English holly are worthwhile but extra special are: 'Pyramidalis' Neat, pyramidal outline, good berries. '**Madame Briot**' Leaves boldly edged with gold; red berries. '**Ferox Argentea**' Male, with prickles all over the surface of the silver and green leaves.

LIRIODENDRON TULIPIFERA
'FASTIGIATUM' Tulip tree

A tulip tree for smaller gardens. The branches are held erect and the flowers, on mature trees, are greenish with rusty insides. Best as a lone specimen.
HEIGHT Large. CULTIVATION Sun. Most soils. HARDINESS 4.

MAGNOLIA

A large group of trees with plenty of choice for smaller gardens.
HEIGHT Small, medium or large.
CULTIVATION Shade or dappled shade. Most soils, not too dry. Some are lime-haters.
HARDINESS 4.

M. x *loebneri* 'Leonard Messel' Medium tree, pink flowers in spring. Lime-tolerant.
M. x *soulangeana* Medium to large tree with pink-tinged large white flowers, in spring. Less happy on lime, but tolerates it.
M. stellata Small to medium tree, starry white flowers produced early in the year.

MALUS Apple

Large group of ornamental trees, many of them well suited to heavy or difficult soils. Attractive blossom and good outline.
HEIGHT Small to medium. CULTIVATION Sun. Most soils. HARDINESS 4.
M. 'Hillieri' Medium-sized, smothered in pink flowers which open white.
M. 'John Downie' Colourful fruits (red and yellow) in autumn.

PRUNUS Cherry, plum, almond, cherry laurel

Huge, choice genus from small evergreen shrubs to large deciduous trees. Blossom in shades of pink or white.
HEIGHT Small, medium or large.
CULTIVATION Sun or dappled shade. Most soils. HARDINESS 4.
P. avium and other hybrid cherries.
P. sargentii Pink blossom, fiery autumn colour.
P. 'Shirofugen' Spreading branches, pink flowers, late, with the emerging foliage.
P. 'Shirotae' Spreading branches, white blossom, early.
P. 'Umineko' A small, upright cherry with white flowers and rusty golden-yellow autumn foliage.
P. dulcis Almond. Rich pink blossom in very early spring.

ROBINIA PSEUDOACACIA 'FRISIA'
False acacia

A golden form of false acacia with foliage that retains its golden hue all summer. Benefits from a sheltered spot.

HEIGHT small to medium. CULTIVATION Sun. Most soils. HARDINESS 4.
'Casque Rouge' Pink-flowered species with brittle branches and ferny, pinnate foliage.

SOPHORA JAPONICA 'PENDULA'
Japanese pagoda tree

A fine outline tree shaped, in maturity, like an upturned glass, its outer stems actually touching the ground.
HEIGHT Medium. CULTIVATION Shade or dappled shade. Most soils, not too dry.
HARDINESS 4.

SORBUS Rowan, whitebeam

Large genus of mostly small or medium trees with white or cream flowers and copious berries in wide range of shades.
HEIGHT Small to medium. CULTIVATION Sun or dappled shade. Most soils.
HARDINESS 4.
S. aucuparia Pinnate foliage; red, orange, yellow, pink or white berries.
S. vilmorinii Refined foliage, pink berries.
S.cashmiriana Best grown as a multi-trunked shrub; has pink blossom followed by large, pure white berries.
S. 'Joseph Rock' Especially good for autumn colour: its leaves turn purplish-bronze, contrasting with the amber berries.

SORBUS CASHMIRIANA

INDEX

Page numbers in *italic* indicate illustrations. Page numbers in **bold** indicate an entry in the Great Plant Guide.